Better Homes and Gardens®

EMBROIDERY

BETTER HOMES AND GARDENS® BOOKS

Editor: Gerald Knox
Art Director: Ernest Shelton
Associate Art Director: Randall Yontz
Production and Copy Editors: David Kirchner, Paul Kitzke
Crafts Editor: Nancy Lindemeyer
Senior Crafts Editor—Books: Joan Cravens
Associate Crafts Editor: Ann Levine
Senior Graphic Designer: Harijs Priekulis
Embroidery Book Designers: Faith Berven, Neoma Alt West
Graphic Designers: Sheryl Veenschoten, Rich Lewis, Linda Ford

---

CONTENTS

Mastery of only a few basic stitches is all that is required to make the projects in this splendid collection of embroidery from around the world. Each bold, imaginative design is a joy to stitch in yarns, floss, or pearl cotton. And for each project, we include complete step-by-step instructions and patterns, as well as directions for the final assembly.

In this section are needlework treasures from days gone by, including counted-thread stitcheries, white-on-white embroidery, and cutwork. And to bring the designs up-to-date, we have simplified the instructions and included tips on hemstitching and other fine finishing techniques.

Our treasure chest of motifs from nature includes embroidery and crewelwork projects featuring wild-flowers, butterflies, and a beautiful woodland fantasy wall hanging.

Cross-Stitch and Counted-Thread Techniques _____ 48-65

To help you develop your skill in this traditional embroidery technique, we present stitcheries worked in cross-stitch and other challenging counted-thread techniques, such as Hardanger cutwork and blackwork embroidery.

Machine Embroidery _____ 66-75

Machine embroidery is a relatively new stitchery technique. To get you started, we have included some basic machine-embroidery how-to and a variety of easy-to-challenging projects that you can make, regardless of the make or model of your sewing machine.

Special Stitchery Techniques _____ 76-89

Working with metal threads, stitching with a hook instead of a needle, and using mirrors and shells—all will make your embroideries interesting and exciting. You will find each of these techniques in this chapter—plus a wonderfully creative sampler.

Glossary _____ 90-96

Here are drawings of individual embroidery stitches and some basic how-to information to help you in all your stitchery projects.

Folk Embroidery

What better way to begin a book about embroidery than with vibrant designs from many different cultures! When you stitch one of these folk embroideries, you will capture the essence of this creative art as it is practiced around the world. The bold motifs on this tablecloth are an appropriate reflection of the happy, exuberant spirit of folk stitchery. In other sections of our book, you will find beautiful projects to make in a variety of techniques that represent the heritage of generations of needleworkers.

So, whether you are an accomplished stitcher or a beginner, you will find much to interest you in this step-by-step guide to many unique, challenging, and useful embroidery projects. Select from our robust section of folk embroidery, or pick a project from our treasure chest of old-fashioned stitchery. If you'd like to be even more adventuresome, try a new, exciting technique such as machine embroidery. Whatever you choose, you'll find complete instructions, clear illustrations, and a definitive stitch guide. For how-to instructions for this tablecloth, see page 19.

Cross-Stitch Table Runner

Shaded like a mosaic, this cross-stitch design is from the Balkans.

Materials

26x44 inches white #22-count linen, Hardanger, or similar even-weave fabric

Embroidery floss in black, red, orange, light blue, variegated blue, and variegated brown

Small tapestry needle

Graph paper (10 squares per inch)

Directions

To make a colored diagram, use colored pencils to transfer the design below to graph paper. The pattern shown is for one quarter of the corner design and the border motif. Complete the design by reversing the pattern and matching the adjoining sides.

Work the border motif at the lower right of the chart only on the arms of the main motif that extend along the sides of the cloth. Do not work it on the arms that extend toward the lower edges or on the cross in the center of the cloth.

Begin the embroidery by marking a point in one corner of the fabric 6½ inches from two edges. This is the center of the first cross. Stitch with 2 strands of floss throughout, and embroider the cross-stitches first. Work each stitch over 2 threads of the fabric, laying stitches in the spaces between threads. Use a tapestry needle to avoid splitting the threads.

When cross-stitch areas are filled, outline the center octagon and the arms of the cross with black double-running stitches. Omit the black outline around the red octagon. (See the Glossary on pages 90 to 93 for an explanation of the stitches.)

Follow the color key below. When colors are indicated with a slash between them, such as O/B, use the color to the left of the slash (O) in the first and third quadrants of the cross, and the color to the right (B) in the second and fourth quadrants.

Work the border motif for about 24 inches down the length of the cloth, and then repeat the corner motif. Work the border about 5 inches along the short sides, then repeat the corner. Continue completely around the edge of the runner.

Finally, find the exact center of the completed stitchery frame (by counting threads) and repeat the cross motif. Be sure to match the center of the fabric to the center of the design.

Finish with a narrow hem about 5 inches below the border. Work hemstitching, if desired, following instructions on page 26.

Color Key

X   Black
R   Red
O   Orange
P   Light blue
B   Variegated blue
V   Variegated brown

One square equals one stitch over 2 threads. Outline shapes indicated above with black double-running stitches over 2 threads.

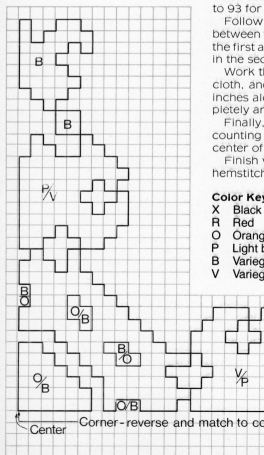

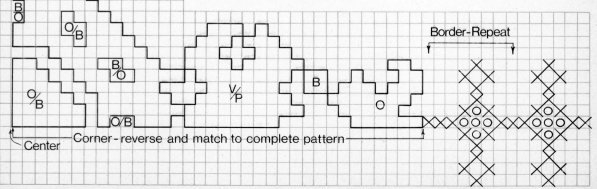

Rustic Wall Hanging

Like many folk embroideries, this Central European wall hanging is made of simple stitches worked into a lively, stylized design. Variable-width yarns give it a bold, contemporary look as well. With the knotted fringe, finished dimensions are 22x26 inches.

Materials
18x23 inches dark green wool
18x23 inches lining fabric
Knitting worsted yarn in bright orange, yellow, and red
Heavy, variable-width (thick-and-thin) knitting or weaving yarns in bronze, burnt orange, gold, red, light yellow, and greenish-yellow
Sewing thread to match variable-width yarns
Dark green sewing thread
Needles
Embroidery hoop (optional)
Plastic or metal curtain rings

Color Key
O   Orange knitting worsted
Y   Yellow knitting worsted
RK   Red knitting worsted
B   Bronze heavy yarn
BO   Burnt orange heavy yarn
G   Gold heavy yarn
R   Red heavy yarn
LY   Light yellow heavy yarn
GY   Greenish-yellow heavy yarn

Directions
Enlarge the pattern, opposite, reversing it for the left side of the design; transfer it, centered, to green wool. Directions for enlarging and transferring designs are on page 95.

Mount the fabric in an embroidery hoop, if desired.

Work the design in straight, lazy daisy, fly, and couching stitches (refer to the Glossary on pages 90 to 93 for an explanation of the stitches). Use knitting worsteds for straight and lazy daisy stitches, shown on the pattern as short lines and loops. Use heavy, variable-width yarns for couching. When filling the inside of shapes, such as tulips, lay couched threads close together so they cover the background fabric. Couch with regular thread in a color to match yarn, making small overcast stitches every ¼ inch. Work the border in bronze fly stitches.

Avoid bulky knots by couching the ends of each strand of yarn to the back of the fabric with dark green sewing thread.

Block the finished embroidery according to the instructions on page 78. Then, with right sides facing, sew together the wool and lining in a ½-inch seam, leaving one side open for turning. Clip corners, turn, and slip-stitch the opening. Add knotted fringe along the lower edge using 25-inch lengths of burnt orange yarn. Sew curtain rings to the upper back for hanging.

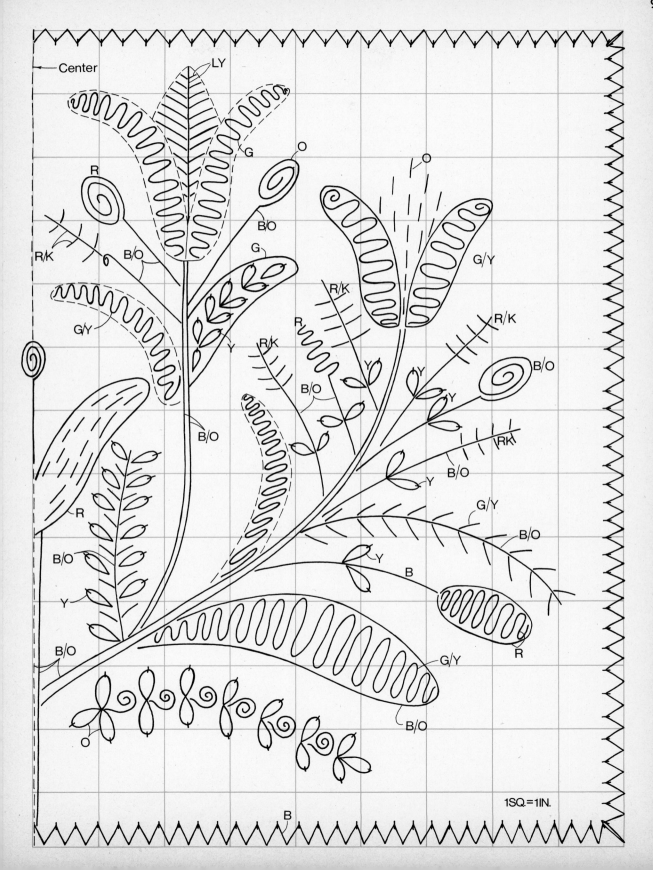

Flowered Tablecloth

Floral motifs are traditionally popular embroidery patterns. These blossoms are outlined in black and sparkle like stained glass. Here, they accent a Central European tablecloth.

Materials

Sufficient even-weave fabric for your cloth (see note below)
Embroidery floss in black, yellow, red, blue, and green
Embroidery needle
Embroidery hoop or frame

Directions

Note: Our tablecloth is 36 inches square, with the motif embroidered in one corner. On a larger cloth, you may wish to work the motif in all four corners.

Enlarge the pattern below and transfer it to the fabric, following the directions on page 95. Insert the fabric into an embroidery hoop or frame so that it will not pucker as you work.

If you wish to pad the dots and satin-stitched areas of the design to give them a rich, raised look, see the directions on page 24. Outline those sections that are to be padded, and pad-stitch them before you begin.

Work the design with 3 strands of floss, following the color and stitch keys on the diagram. After filling in the colored areas of the flowers, outline the dots and flower sections in black outline stitches. Work stems in outline stitches. (For an explanation of the stitches, see the Glossary on pages 90 to 93.)

Block the finished embroidery by steam-pressing it lightly on the wrong side over a padded board.

Machine-stitch 2 inches from the raw edge of the cloth using regular thread in a color to match the fabric. Work a single row of black overcast stitches next to the line of machine stitching. Fringe the fabric between the overcast stitches and the raw edge as shown in the photograph opposite.

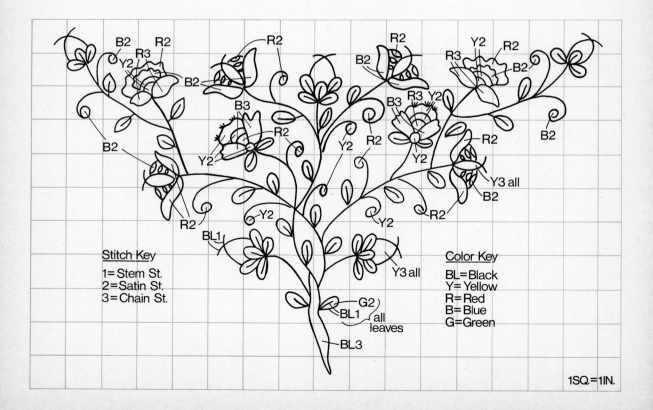

Stitch Key

1 = Stem St.
2 = Satin St.
3 = Chain St.

Color Key

BL = Black
Y = Yellow
R = Red
B = Blue
G = Green

1 SQ. = 1 IN.

Embroidered Crèche

Embroidered in sampler-like stitches, these crèche figures are just as beautiful and impressive as those gowned in satin and haloed in gold.

To capture the vitality of old-world needlework, we embroidered the familiar hearts and flowers motifs in red and green crewel wool. Needlepoint canvas makes cross-stitching the borders and facial features easy. Halos are made of purchased crochet trim, and the completed figures are stuffed with beans or seeds for stability.

Materials

⅜ yard off-white linen or other coarsely woven fabric
1 small skein each of red and green Persian yarn
Embroidery and tapestry needles
6-inch square of cardboard
Embroidery hoop
⅔ yard 1½-inch-wide crocheted lace
White glue
Scraps of #5-mesh mono-canvas
Seeds or beans
Funnel
Scraps of quilt batting or polyester fiberfill

Directions

Enlarge the pattern pieces, following directions on page 95, and transfer the *outlines only* to the wrong side of the fabric. Allow at least 1 inch between each pattern piece (actual seam allowances are ⅜ inch) and keep the patterns far enough away from the edge of the material to allow you to use an embroidery hoop easily. Do not cut out the pattern pieces until the embroidery is finished.

Trace the embroidery details onto the right side of the fabric and mount it in a hoop or frame. Referring to the photograph for colors, satin-stitch the hearts, flowers, and leaves, and stem-stitch the flower stems and hands. Edge Mary's robe with chain stitches and French knots. Joseph's robe has two rows of chain stitches separated by flowers worked in detached chain stitches.

Use 1 strand of yarn for the embroidery.

Work the features and the rows along the base of each figure in cross-stitches, using scraps of needlepoint canvas as a guide. Pin the canvas in position and work the stitches over it. Then dampen the canvas to relax the sizing in it, snip the canvas threads, and gently pull them out one at a time.

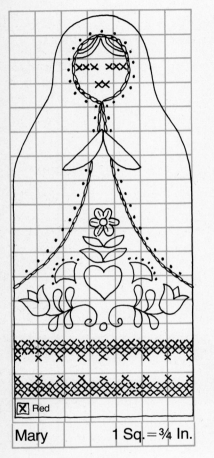

Mary   1 Sq. = ¾ In.

☒ Red

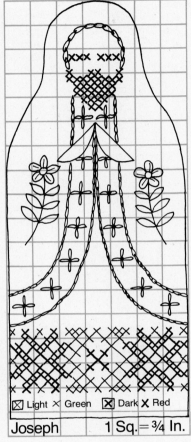

Joseph   1 Sq. = ¾ In.

☒ Light   ✕ Green   ☒ Dark   ✕ Red

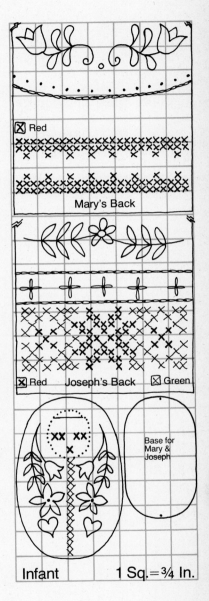

☒ Red

Mary's Back

☒ Red   Joseph's Back   ☒ Green

Base for Mary & Joseph

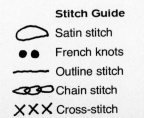

Infant   1 Sq. = ¾ In.

Cut out pattern pieces, leaving ⅜-inch seam allowances. Cut a linen backing for the infant, using the front as a pattern. Sew fronts to backs, leaving Mary and Joseph open along the bottom and leaving a 2-inch opening in the infant. Clip curves and turn right side out. Press a ⅜-inch hem along the bottom edge.

Cut two cardboard bases for Mary and Joseph. Place cardboard on fabric and trace around edges. Cut out fabric bases, adding a ⅜-inch seam allowance. Glue the fabric bases to the cardboard bases, clipping and turning back the raw edges of the fabric.

Place the side seams of the figures at the dots on the bases and sew the edges to the bases, leaving a 2-inch opening on each.

Insert a funnel into the openings and fill the figures as full as possible with seeds or beans. Slip-stitch Mary's and Joseph's openings. Finish stuffing the infant with batting, then slip-stitch.

Stand Mary and Joseph upright, open the seams along the top of each head, and stuff tightly with batting. Slip-stitch openings.

Gather three 8-inch pieces of crocheted lace for halos and tack onto the heads of the figures.

Stitch Guide

⌒ Satin stitch

●● French knots

— — Outline stitch

⟨⟨⟩⟩ Chain stitch

✕✕✕ Cross-stitch

Chain Stitch Pillow

Charmingly stylized animals are also popular motifs in folk stitchery. Who can resist this rooster from Afghanistan with his simple lines, bright colors, and homey appeal?

Directions here are for chain stitches with a needle. To learn how to make them with a crochet hook — called tambour work — turn to page 80.

Materials

18x18 inches black linen or
   cotton
18x18 inches navy or black
   unclipped corduroy
#8 pearl cotton in white, yellow,
   red, green, maroon, and blue
Embroidery needle
Embroidery hoop (optional)
Pillow stuffing

Color Key

W White
Y Yellow
R Red
G Green
M Maroon
B Blue

Directions

This design is composed of a single motif surrounded by a border and repeated 4 times. Recreate the design as shown, or if you prefer, work it just once for a smaller pillow or a wall hanging.

Enlarge the pattern and transfer it to the linen fabric, following the directions on page 95 for enlarging a design without a grid. Work the entire design in chain stitches, following the color key.

When colors are indicated with a slash between them, such as G/B, use the color to the left of the slash (G) in the first and third quadrants, and the color to the right (B) in the second and fourth quadrants, as shown in the photograph.

Begin the embroidery by outlining each block of color with a single row of chain stitches. Then fill in the remainder of the shape with additional rows of chain stitches worked parallel to the outline. Work from the outside of each shape toward the center. For example, embroider the outer edges of the flower shapes first. Then begin filling the petals with rows of chain stitches until you reach the center of the flower, when the chain stitches should be worked in a spiral, as indicated on the pattern.

Block the finished embroidery and stitch the front to the back, right side together, in a ½-inch seam around 3 sides. Turn and stuff the pillow cover, and slip-stitch the fourth side closed.

Cross-Stitch Runner

This floral runner is from Yugoslavia. Work it in the colors shown, or use threads that match your own decor.

Materials

24x40 inches of #22-count Hardanger or other even-weave fabric

Embroidery floss in dark forest green, medium kelly green, and orange

Embroidery needle

Embroidery hoop (optional)

Graph paper (10 squares per inch)

Colored pencils to match floss

Color and Stitch Key

Cross Stitch	Backstitch
■ Dark Green	∣ Orange
× Med. Green	⚡ Dark Green
○ Orange	

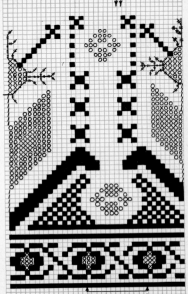

Remaining border repeat Center repeat

Border repeat

Directions

To make a colored diagram, use colored pencils to transfer the chart below to graph paper. Use sufficient paper to work out the pattern repeat across the short end of the runner.

To work the embroidery, first find the center of the narrow ends of the fabric. Allowing 2½ inches of plain fabric for hemming, begin working the pattern from the center toward the outer edges. Work each stitch over 2 threads of fabric. Note that the center motif is slightly different from the others. Work this motif only once, then repeat the design that is shown on the left in the chart. The line of backstitches in the center of each motif is a single row; it is not repeated when the pattern is reversed.

When you have finished stitching the motifs along the end of the runner, continue working the side borders to a length of about 35 inches—less if you prefer. Then turn the corner and work the floral motifs across the opposite end of the runner.

Finish your runner with a plain hem or a row of hemstitching, following directions on page 26.

Embroidered Throw and Floor Pillows

This throw and the matching floor pillows, stitched with crewel wools, feature a sampling of symbolic American Indian motifs.

Materials

1 twin-size gray utility blanket
Twelve 40-yard skeins 3-ply black Persian wool yarn
Three 40-yard skeins 3-ply light gray Persian wool yarn
Three 40-yard skeins 3-ply brownish-red Persian wool
2 large-eyed darning needles
Large embroidery hoop
3⅝ yards black cotton (lining)
1 roll quilt batting (blanket)
Polyester fiberfill (pillows)
#8 black pearl cotton

Stitch Guide

1—Roumanian stitch
2—Satin stitch
3—Couching stitch
4—Laid work
5—Star stitch
6—Buttonhole stitch

Color Key

A Black
B Gray
C Red

Directions

Embroider the throw with 9 motifs separated by "goose track" borders. Arrange motifs from left to right in 3 rows as follows: row 1: motifs A, B, and C; row 2: D, E, and F; row 3: G, H, and I. Patterns are below and on page 18.

Enlarge the patterns, following directions on page 95. Transfer each design to a 20x20-inch piece of tissue paper and pin the patterns to the blanket. Note that each motif has a 1-inch border around it—making a 2-inch border between motifs when they are transferred to the fabric.

Cut the blanket into a 62-inch square. Using hand or machine basting, transfer the patterns to the fabric. Be sure to include the outlines for the borders. Tear away the tissue paper before you begin the embroidery. Work with fabric in a hoop to prevent puckering.

Using the basting stitches as a guide, work the embroidery with 5-foot lengths of yarn threaded into a large, sharp needle and doubled. Follow the color and stitch keys for the motifs. If you are using a heavier yarn, such as rug yarn, do not double it and buy only half as much. (Refer to the Glossary on pages 90 to 93 for an explanation of the stitches.)

After completing the motifs, remove the basting stitches and steam-press each design with a warm iron. Make sure basted lines for borders are straight and approximately 2 inches apart.

Work the borders in black buttonhole stitches, with three "tracks" positioned every inch (see diagram on page 18). Work the two inner vertical borders first, going from top to bottom. Then work the inner horizontal borders, carrying the yarn under the fabric at each square's corner where the borders meet. Work the inside line of border stitches around the blanket's edge so that the loops of the stitches are 2 inches from the edge. Press gently.

To quilt, lay the blanket face down and stretch a layer of batting over it, trimming any excess. Piece the lining fabric to make a 66-inch square, and lay it on top of the quilt batting. Allow a 2-inch margin around each edge. Pin the three layers together.

Tie the layers together with black pearl cotton at 3-inch intervals along the border of each square. To tie, insert the needle through the

continued

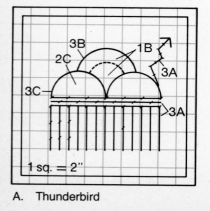

A. Thunderbird

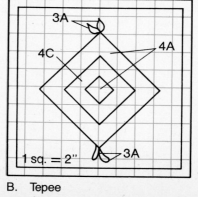

B. Tepee

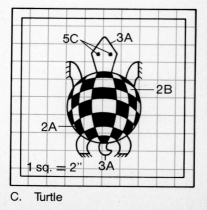

C. Turtle

Embroidered Throw and Floor Pillows *(continued)*

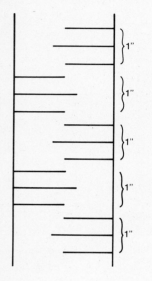

throw from back to front, and take a small stitch on the front side under an embroidered stitch. Pull the thread through to the lining side and double-knot it. Continue along each border on the inside of the throw and around the edges.

After tying, trim the lining to ⅝ inch beyond the edge of the throw. Fold this margin in half and fold again *over* the edge to the front. Miter the corners. Pin but do not stitch.

Add the final line of outer border stitches using a blanket stitch and working through all three layers. Finally, secure the binding by slip-stitching the edge of the lining to the front of the throw with black sewing thread.

Pillows: *Note:* Cut the remaining blanket fabric in half to make two pillow fronts. Enlarge patterns for any two motifs and transfer them to the blanket pieces. Center the designs on the fabric, and enlarge the border to 2 inches. Baste along the design lines, and embroider as for the throw.

Cut back pieces from black lining fabric. With right sides together, stitch front and back together in a ⅝-inch seam. Leave an opening for turning. Stuff the pillows with polyester fiberfill and slip-stitch the openings closed.

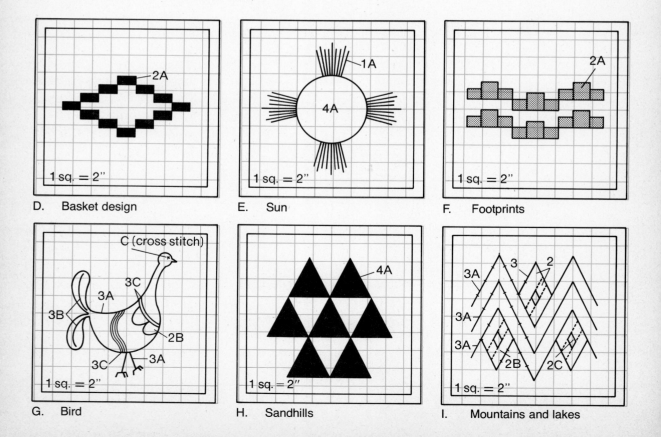

D.   Basket design

E.   Sun

F.   Footprints

G.   Bird

H.   Sandhills

I.   Mountains and lakes

Hungarian Cloth *(shown on pages 4 and 5)*

Directions

The pattern is for one quarter of the tablecloth. Enlarge it according to directions on page 95, reversing it as necessary to complete the design, and transfer it to the fabric. Mount the fabric in a hoop or frame, if you wish.

Anchor the thread end with a waste-knot (directions are on page 51), and work the entire design in buttonhole stitches. When working the flower petals, centers, and dots, lay the stitches side-by-side, with the loop part of each stitch along the outer edge of the shape, as shown on the petals below. Work stems, scallops, scrolls, and the straight line along the border in double buttonhole stitches, as shown on the stem below. (For an explanation of this stitch, see the Glossary on pages 90 to 93.)

When the embroidery is finished, block it according to the directions on page 78. Turn up a narrow hem and add purchased crocheted edging. Or work a narrow band of hemstitching over 1 or 2 drawn threads, following directions on page 26. Then add a lace edge crocheted from the red embroidery thread for the scalloped edge, following the directions at right.

You needn't be a long-experienced stitcher to work beautiful embroideries. This Hungarian cloth, with its bold, floral motif and scallops, is worked entirely in one stitch.

Materials

1¼ yards of off-white linen or linen-like fabric, or any length suitable for your table.
#5 pearl cotton in red
Embroidery needle
Embroidery hoop (optional)
Purchased red crocheted edging or size 7 crochet hook (to make your own edging)

Scalloped Edge

Row 1: Make sc with ch 1 between around entire cloth. End with sl st in first sc.

Row 2: *2 sc in first ch 1 sp, 2 hdc in next sp, 2 dc in next sp, 2 trc in next sp, 2 dc in next sp, 2 hdc in next sp, 2 sc in next sp, 2 sl st in next sp. Repeat from * around cloth. End with sl st in first sc.

1 sq. = 1″

Old-Fashioned Stitchery

Experience a bit of nostalgia by stitching some of our charming old-fashioned designs. Embroidering in the manner of yesteryear can be refreshing and exciting. And to help you re-create these treasured old-time designs, we have simplified your work with easy to follow step-by-step instructions. All of the stitches are explained in the Glossary beginning on page 90, and each project is explained with patterns and graphs.

So if you would like to embroider a design from the past, select a project from this section with that special look of days gone by. Directions for the cloth shown here are on page 32.

Blue Rose Tablecloth

The heirloom tablecloth shown here is stitched in a form of counted thread work. The rose motif is embroidered using a straight stitch, while the openwork borders and hemstitching are simple drawn thread work.

Materials

Purchased even-weave tablecloth or even-weave linen yardage of desired length
Thread to match fabric
#5 pearl cotton in light, medium, and dark blue
Embroidery needle
Embroidery hoop or frame
Graph paper (optional)
Colored pencils (optional)

Color Key

O Light blue
X Medium blue
△ Dark blue

Directions

The rose motif and openwork border are embroidered once in the center of each side of our tablecloth. The pattern may be worked on any size square or rectangular tablecloth or runner, and repeated as often as you wish.

Our tablecloth is worked on #36-count even-weave linen, and each motif measures approximately 3¼x13 inches. A fabric with a different count (number of threads per inch) will yield a rose of a different size. For example, on #22-count Hardanger fabric, the motif will be about 1½ times larger than on #36-count fabric.

Before plotting out the design for the cloth itself, you might want to embroider one complete motif either with or without the drawn thread border on a scrap of the fabric you intend to use for your tablecloth. In this way, you will be able to determine exactly what size the motif will be on the fabric you have chosen.

The graphed pattern below represents the center rose motif and the oblong extension to one side of it. For a complete pattern, reverse the oblong motif, match it to the center at the points indicated, and repeat it on the other side of the rose.

The proportions of the pattern as shown on the graph are deceiving. Each square on the graph actually represents a long, thin straight stitch, even though we have used squares to indicate each stitch in order to include color indications for the pattern. If you find working from a colored graph easier, you may wish to transfer the design to graph paper with colored pencils.

Embroider the entire design in straight stitches. (If you are unfamiliar with this stitch, see the Glossary.) Work each stitch over 7 threads of the fabric and leave 2 threads between each stitch. Except in the top row, the top of each stitch is worked into the same space as the bottom of the stitch in the row above.

To work the rose motif once in the center of each side of your tablecloth as we did, begin by finding the exact center of each side of the cloth. Mark it with a tailor's tack about 5 inches above the raw edge. Then begin working the rose, starting in the center. After you have finished the rose, work the drawn thread box and border, following the directions on the next page.

continued

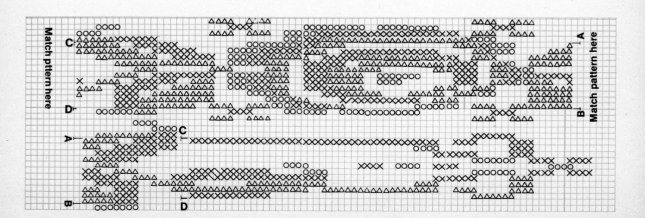

Blue Rose Tablecloth *(continued)*

For the drawn thread work, first plan for the ends of the box to fall about ¾ inch beyond the ends of the rose motif, with the sides about ⅝ inch above and below the sides of the motif.

From the fabric, withdraw about 6 threads that run parallel to the hem (making the drawn area about ¼ inch wide if your fabric is #36-count linen). Then, with thread to match your fabric, bind the remaining (vertical) threads in groups of 4, using the same stitch used for hemstitching. (For hemstitching how-to, see page 26.)

Bind both edges of the drawn area, creating a "ladder" of threads around the rose motif.

Then find the center of the short sides of the box and withdraw an additional 6 threads to make the border that extends around the cloth to join the boxes. In the corners of the drawn area, where warp and weft threads are both withdrawn, work buttonhole stitches to stabilize the edges of the fabric and prevent raveling.

Finish the cloth with a double row of decorative hemstitching. Or simply turn up the raw edge ¼ inch, then turn it up again and press. Blindstitch for a plain. tailored hem.

For A Fine Finish—Outlining and Padding

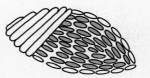

It is time-consuming to outline and pad design areas to be covered with close, fine stitches. But when you take time for this extra step, the result is striking. We recommend you make it a regular preliminary part of your embroidery.

Outlining and padding design elements gives your embroidery neat, crisp edges and lovely rounded surfaces; it enables you to highlight important motifs; and it strengthens raw edges on pieces of cutwork—all hallmarks of fine handiwork.

For both outlining and padding, use the same color thread as you intend to use for the finishing step. You may use exactly the same thread, or you might want to try a slightly coarser and more tightly twisted thread for a firmer edge.

Begin by working an outline around each shape with small running stitches, backstitches, or split stitches. (See the Glossary on pages 90 to 93 for stitch how-to.)

Except on dots or small circles, pad with double running stitches worked back and forth across the shape (parallel to the outline) as shown in the top diagram at left.

Or pad with a cord (or group of cords) laid underneath fine satin or buttonhole stitches, as in the center diagram at left.

For dots or small circles, fill in the outline and pad the center with a single double cross-stitch or star stitch, depending on the size of the circle and the thickness of your thread (see lower diagram at left).

Embroidered Pansy Cloth

Directions

Mark but do not cut out a 52-inch circle on the fabric. Following directions on page 95, enlarge the pattern and transfer four pansy clusters to the fabric, spacing them equally around the circle. Add a single pansy motif midway between each cluster. Match the hemline on the pattern to the circle on the fabric.

Work the embroidery in a hoop, using 1 strand of floss throughout. Work leaves and stems in medium blue outline stitches. Use medium blue floss to satin-stitch around the pansies, *except* where petals extend beyond the rim of the cloth. Work these extensions in buttonhole stitches. In the centers of the flowers, work four circles in white satin stitches with a yellow French knot in the middle. Lines radiating from the center are light blue (outline stitches), as are the French knots on each flower.

To finish the cloth, cut away the fabric from the buttonhole-stitched edges of the pansies using small, sharp scissors. Trim remaining fabric to ½ inch below the hem. Turn up a narrow hem and add crocheted edging.

Clusters of pansies on graceful stems and a crocheted edging border this circular linen tablecloth. Embroidered in simple stitches even a beginner will be familiar with, it has a romantic, old-fashioned look.

Materials

54x54 inches white linen or fine percale
Embroidery floss in white, yellow, and medium and light cornflower blue
Embroidery needle
Embroidery hoop or frame
Blue and white crocheted edging, ½ inch wide

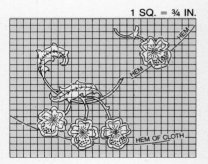

1 SQ. = ¾ IN.

Cross-Stitch Rose Wreaths

Here are two ways to use this delightful cross-stitch rose wreath design. Create a table runner or make tree ornaments that can double as pin-cushions or sachets.

Materials

Even-weave fabric, such as Aida cloth, Hardanger, or linen (see note below)
#5 pearl cotton in varying shades of red, orange, pink, and green
Tapestry needle
Embroidery hoop
Gold cord
Polyester stuffing

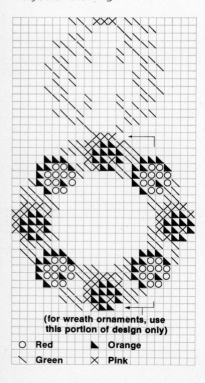

(for wreath ornaments, use this portion of design only)

O	Red	▲	Orange
╲	Green	✕	Pink

Directions

Note: The ornaments are worked on #24-count Hardanger cloth and the motif measures 2 inches across. The runner is worked on #20-count Hardanger and the wreaths measure 2¼ inches in diameter. With different fabric, work a sample to determine size.

Ornaments: Work in three shades of pink and one of green.

Following the graph, work wreath motif, leaving at least 2 inches of fabric between each for border and seams. Embroider several before cutting them out. Cut out wreaths with a 1-inch margin around the design. Cut matching circle for the back. Stitch front and back together ⅜ inch from edge of wreath, leaving a small opening. Turn, press, stuff lightly, and slip-stitch.

Tack gold cord along the edges of the ornament, tie the ends in a bow (slip-stitch to hold), and add a nylon-thread hanger.

Runner: Cut fabric 2 inches larger than the finished runner will be. Ours is 16x48 inches and has four wreaths across the short side and 13 down the length, with smaller, green wreaths between.

Begin with a rose wreath 2½ inches from the raw edge in the center of a long side. Work toward the short ends, connecting rose wreaths with green ones. On corners, work a green wreath at right angles to a rose wreath. Finish with hemstitching.

For a Fine Finish—Hemstitching

Hemstitching adds a nice decorative touch to delicate embroidery and provides a framework for a fringe on finely woven fabrics.

To work this lovely hem, make sure your edge is perfectly straight by removing a thread and cutting the fabric along the channel that is left. Fold under the raw edge, turn up the hem, and baste.

Turn the cloth so the wrong side faces you, and carefully snip 2 to 4 threads parallel to the hem, *directly above the upper fold of the hem.* Hemstitch with a thread the same size and color as the threads in the fabric, following the diagram at left below.

Slip the knotted thread end under the fold and bring the thread through the hem 2 threads below the drawn area. Insert the needle 3 or 4 threads to the right and in the drawn area. Go under 3 or 4 threads and bring it up again still in the drawn area. Then cross over 3 or 4 threads and reinsert the needle, slipping it under the fold and bringing it out again 2 threads below the drawn area. Pull the thread snug, and repeat.

You may wish to add a second row of stitches along the top of the drawn area, wrapping either the same threads as before and creating a ladder (below, center), or wrapping alternate ones (below, right).

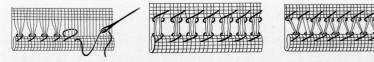

Pillowcases from Aunt Mary's

Beautifully designed and stitched bed linens are among our favorite needlework treasures. The three embroidered pillowcases you see here are heirlooms from the collection of Aunt Mary—a gracious lady who truly loves fine stitchery.

If you don't have someone in your family who hands down elegant, old-fashioned embroideries, create your own with our patterns.

Materials
Pillowcases (see note below)
Sufficient crocheted lace edging
   for hems of cases
Embroidery needles

Flowered cases
Embroidery floss in white,
   yellow, and light and medium
   shades of pink, blue, green,
   and lavender

Lace butterfly cases
White embroidery floss
Nylon net
Small lace medallions, cut from
   doilies or lace yardage

Embroidered butterfly cases
White embroidery floss

Directions
Note: Make pillowcases to fit your pillows, or use purchased cases with hems removed. Shape the lower edge according to the pattern.

General instructions: Enlarge the pattern, reversing it to complete the design, and transfer it to the fabric, following instructions on page 95. Embroider according to directions below.

Turn up a narrow hem on the pillowcases, hemstitching if desired. Finish with crocheted edging sewn along the bottom.

Flowered cases: Use 2 strands of floss. Work stems in shades of green outline stitches; small leaves are green lazy daisy stitches. Work flower petals and large leaves in straight stitches, alternating light and dark shades of floss. Use dark green for the laid work base of one flower. Flower centers are white and yellow French knots.

Lace butterfly cases: With 1 strand of white floss, work flower petals and leaves in padded satin stitches, following directions on page 24. For French knots, use 3 strands. Work stems in outline stitches with 2 strands.

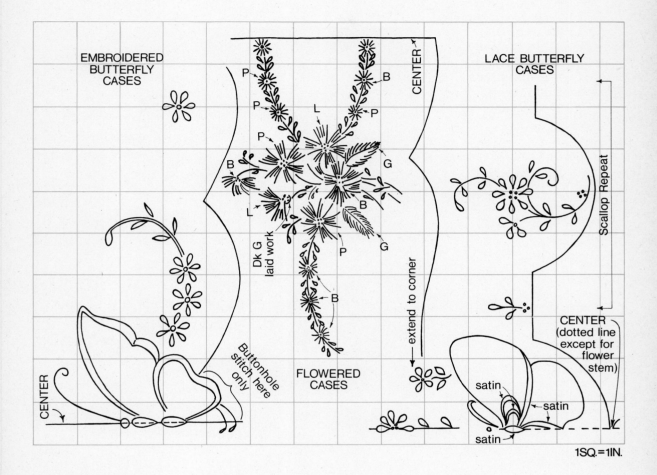

EMBROIDERED BUTTERFLY CASES

LACE BUTTERFLY CASES

CENTER

Scallop Repeat

Dk G laid work

Buttonhole stitch here only

CENTER

FLOWERED CASES

extend to corner

CENTER (dotted line except for flower stem)

satin

satin

satin

1SQ.=1IN.

Aunt Mary's butterfly is a combination of embroidery and needle lace. For a close approximation, work the antennae and the body and wing detail shown on the pattern in satin stitches over a padding thread, with 1 strand of floss. Then, with small, sharp-pointed scissors, cut away the fabric interior of the butterfly. Lay a small piece of fine-mesh nylon netting or organdy behind the design, and buttonhole-stitch the netting to the fabric along the outline of the butterfly, working the thread through both the pillowcase and the sheer fabric. Work additional satin stitches over the body and wing detail to join the two pieces of fabric. Finally, appliqué small pieces of lace to the sheer wings.

Embroidered butterfly cases: Using 1 strand of white floss, work the flowers, leaves, and butterfly outline (except at lower edge) in padded satin stitches (see page 24 for directions for outlining and padding). Work the lower edge of the butterfly in buttonhole stitches to bind the raw edge of the fabric. Work antennae and stems in outline stitches, using 2 strands of floss.

Color Key For Flowered Cases
P Pink
B Blue
L Lavender
G Green

Crewel Picture Frame

Set off your favorite picture in this crewel frame, then adapt the designs to embellish a Christmas stocking.

Materials
21x26 inches white linen or any even-weave fabric
3-ply Persian yarn in light, medium, and dark copen blue
17x22-inch piece of ⅜-inch plywood for backing
Quilt batting
Crewel needle
Tape or staples

Color Key
A   Dark copen blue
B   Medium copen blue
C   Light copen blue

Stitch Key
1   Chain stitch
2   Satin stitch
3   French knots
4   Outline stitch
5   Laid work

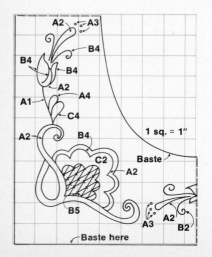

Directions
The pattern at left is for one quadrant of the design. Enlarge it and complete the remaining three quadrants. Extend small flower motifs up sides and across top and bottom, as shown in the photograph. Finally, transfer the design to the fabric.

With regular sewing thread, baste the linen along the inner and outer edges of the frame, as indicated. Embroider the design using 1 strand of yarn and following color and stitch guides. Block the finished embroidery, following directions on page 78.

Cut an oval from the center of the plywood to correspond with the oval on the pattern. Pad wood with 2 to 4 layers of quilt batting and stretch the embroidery over the batting, aligning the basted lines with the frame edges. Cut ovals from the quilt batting and clip the curves on the linen so the fabric lies smoothly.

Tape or staple the linen edges to the back of the frame and mount a picture or mirror in the center.

Blue and White Tea Cozy

Keep your teapot piping hot with this embroidered cozy, lined for extra warmth. The design is an adaptation of the famous blue onion pattern, worked in white on blue linen fabric.

Materials
½ yard blue fabric
½ yard blue lining fabric
6 skeins white embroidery floss
Quilt batting
Embroidery needle
Embroidery hoop or frame
1 yard white covered cable cord

1 SQ.=1IN.

Directions

The pattern at right is for the flowers in the left corner of the tea cozy: enlarge it to size. The flower in the lower right corner is ¾ as large as the lower flower in the diagram, while the one on the upper right is 1½ times as large.

Cut fabric 14x16 inches, fold in half lengthwise, and round top corners slightly. Baste along seam line, 1 inch from the edge, and transfer the design as shown in the photograph to the fabric.

Using 3 strands of floss, work stems and leaf outlines primarily in stem stitches, filling half of some leaves with satin stitches. Work flowers in chain stitches, with satin stitching along the top of the fan-shaped flower. Fill small dots on pattern with French knots. For small flowers, use lazy daisy stitches.

Cut back, lining pieces, and batting to same size as front. Sew cording to front. Sew batting to front and back; stitch back to front. Assemble lining, and tack to the inside of the cover.

Embroidered Tablecloth *(shown on pages 20 and 21)*

This lovely tablecloth is made up of only two motifs repeated on the diagonal. You can duplicate our cloth, or experiment with your own design, using only one motif, for example, for a tablecloth, pillow top, wall hanging, or curtain.

Materials

36x50 inches green linen, or sufficient yardage for your cloth

72 skeins white cotton embroidery floss (or sufficient skeins to complete your cloth)

Embroidery hoop or frame

Embroidery needles

Stitch Key

1. Outline stitch
2. Leaf stitch
3. Herringbone stitch
4. Long-and-short stitch
5. Feather stitch
6. Chain stitch
7. Twisted chain stitch
8. Rosette chain stitch
9. German knot
10. French knot
11. Braid stitch
12. Backstitch
13. Open chain stitch
14. Padded satin stitch
15. Chain scroll stitch
16. Running stitch
17. Lazy daisy French knot
18. Cable stitch
19. Herringbone stitch with feather stitch overlay
20. Buttonhole stitch

Directions

To duplicate our cloth, enlarge the patterns on the next page and transfer them to the fabric, following the placement diagram. Directions for enlarging and transferring designs are on page 95. When enlarged to full size, motif A is about 11 inches wide by 18 inches long, and motif B is about 15 inches wide by 17 inches long. Mount the fabric in a hoop or frame, if desired. If you intend to launder the cloth, we suggest you pre-shrink the fabric and floss beforehand. Soak skeins of thread in warm water for a few minutes and let them dry thoroughly.

Work the design entirely in white floss, using the number of strands indicated in parentheses on the pattern following the stitch numbers. (Directions for all the stitches are in the Glossary.)

When the embroidery is finished, press the cloth lightly on the wrong side, and hem.

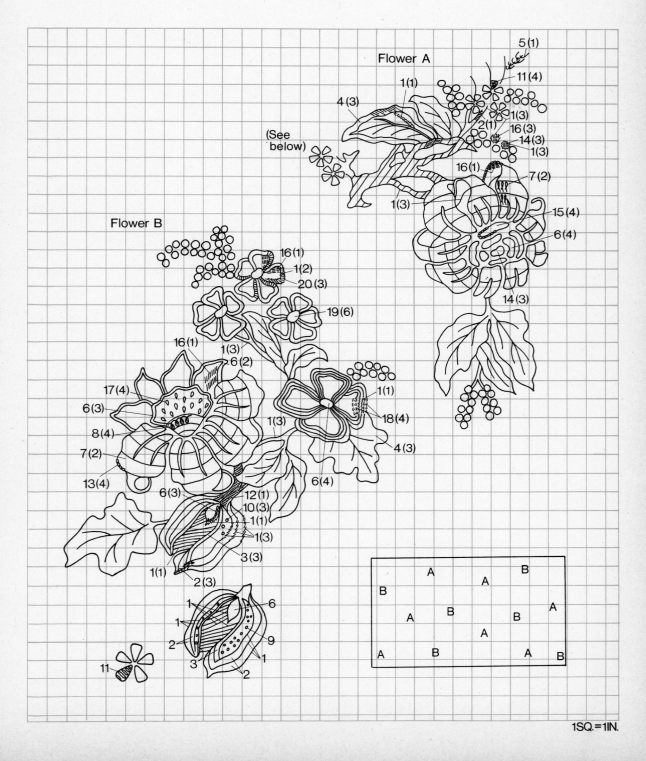

Flower A

5(1)
11(4)
1(1)
4(3)
(See below)
1(3)
2(1)
16(3)
14(3)
1(3)
16(1)
7(2)
1(3)
15(4)
6(4)
14(3)

Flower B

16(1)
1(2)
20(3)
19(6)
16(1)
1(3)
6(2)
17(4)
6(3)
8(4)
7(2)
13(4)
6(3)
1(3)
1(1)
18(4)
4(3)
6(4)
12(1)
10(3)
1(1)
1(3)
3(3)
1(1)
2(3)
1
1
2
3
6
9
1
2
11

		A				B	
B				A			
	A		B			B		A
				A			
A		B				A		B

1SQ.=1IN.

Nature

The world around us is a boundless source of design motifs, and for years, embroiderers have looked upon Mother Nature as master designer. It is hard to imagine more perfect stitchery subjects than a graceful butterfly or the beautifully muted colors and natural symmetry of a delicate flower.

In this section, we offer you a very special selection of designs from nature to stitch in a variety of embroidery techniques.

Whether you delight in crewel yarns or richly colored cotton floss, you are sure to find many must-do projects. These beautiful crewelwork pillows are an excellent example of how an embroiderer can forever capture a moment in nature. For complete instructions for these unique pillows, please see page 46.

Wildflower Pillow and Crewel Throw

You'll enjoy embroidering our crewel throw and forest-green pillow as decorative accessories for your home. With our designs, you can preserve forever the delicate freshness of wildflowers —clover and violets, black-eyed susans, dandelions, and five other patterns.

Use wool and cotton threads, and when your throw is stitched, add a lacy crocheted edging. Patterns are on the following pages.

Wildflower pillow

Materials
1 yard of green velveteen
5 yards of cable cord
#5 pearl cotton in white, blue, brown, red, medium and light pink, medium and light green, medium and light violet, medium and light orange, and dark, medium, and light yellow
Transfer pencil
Tissue paper
Embroidery hoop or frame (see note below)
Embroidery needle
Pillow stuffing, or 14-inch circular box-pillow form

Directions
Note: Use a hoop larger than the diameter of the finished project to avoid crushing the nap.

On tissue paper, draw a 14-inch circle. Using a scale of "1 square equals ¼ inch," enlarge the patterns on pages 38 and 39. Trace flowers at random on the paper pattern, referring to the photograph for placement suggestions. Scatter flowers to avoid large empty spaces in the circle.

Using the transfer pencil, trace flowers on the front of the pattern. Then iron the pattern on the back of the fabric so the design will be face up when embroidered. Iron lightly over a padded surface, such as a terry cloth towel, to avoid crushing the nap. Go over design lines with chalk if they are hard to see.

Hand-baste along outlines of motifs so you can embroider them from the right side. Otherwise embroidery must be worked from the back of the fabric.

Cut out the fabric circle, leaving an additional 2-inch margin around it so the fabric can be held securely in a hoop.

Embroider the flowers, following the stitch and color guides on pages 38 and 39. (Refer to the Glossary on pages 90 to 93 for an explanation of the stitches.)

When the embroidery is finished, press the wrong side on a padded surface. Steam lightly to avoid crushing the nap.

Cover cording with strips of velveteen cut on the bias, or use purchased cording in a matching or contrasting color. Pin the cording along the edge of the 14-inch circle, and machine-stitch with a zipper foot.

Cut a 3-inch-wide strip of fabric for boxing, and stitch it to the cording, right sides together, in a ½-inch seam. Sew a second row of cording ½ inch from the edge of the other side of the strip.

Cut a 15-inch circle of fabric for the pillow back, and pin it to the boxing strip, right sides together. Using a zipper foot, stitch along the cording seam, leaving 12 inches open. Turn right side out, insert the pillow form, and slip-stitch the opening.

Wildflower Afghan

Materials
2 yards of 44-inch-wide white wool
16 oz. of Spinnerin sweater and afghan yarn to match fabric
Small skeins of Persian yarn in 6 shades of green, 5 shades of orange, 4 shades of blue, 3 shades of violet, and 2 shades of pink, brown and yellow
Transfer pencil
Tissue paper
Embroidery hoop
Crewel embroidery needle
Size 0 crochet hook

Directions
Draw a 14-inch circle on paper. Enlarge the patterns on the next page (scale is "1 square equals ½ inch"), and draw each wildflower inside the circle once. Retrace the *front* of the flower with a transfer pencil and then transfer the designs to the *wrong* side of the fabric. Center the circle of flowers in one corner of the wool, keeping the designs about 9 inches from the raw edges.

Using regular thread in a contrasting color, baste around outlines so you can work on the face of the fabric.

Embroider the designs, using 2 strands of wool for all the stitches except the French knots. Use 3 strands for French knots. Follow the stitch and color guides given with the patterns on the next page.

Finish the afghan with the 5-inch crocheted border, following directions below. Or add a 5-inch fringe.

Crocheted Border
First scallop: Starting at center of scallop, ch 20; join with sl st to first ch to form ring. Work 30 sc in ring, join with sl st to first sc. Work back and forth in rows. *Row 1:* Ch 5, (sk next sc, dc in next sc, ch 2) 5 times; sk next sc. Work (dc, ch 3, dc) in next sc, (ch 2, sk next sc, dc in next sc) 6 times. Ch 1, turn. *Row 2:* Sc in first dc, (2 sc in next ch-2 sp, sc in next dc) 6 times; 3 sc in ch-3 sp at tip of scallop, sc in next dc, (2 sc in next ch-2 sp, sc in next dc) 5 times, ending with 3 sc over turning ch. Ch 1, turn. *Row 3:* Sk first sc, sc in each sc to center sc at tip of scallop, 3 sc in center sc, sc in each sc to end. Working as for Row 3, work Rows 4, 5, 6, and 7. *Row 8:* Sl st in first sc, ch 4, tr in same sc, (ch 3, sk 2 sc, holding back the last lp of each tr, work 2 tr in next sc, yo and draw through 3 lps on hook—tr-cluster made) 7 times; ch 3, (work tr-cluster, ch 3, and tr-cluster in center sc), (ch 3, sk 2 sc, tr-cluster in next sc) 8 times. Ch 1, turn. *Row 9:* Work (sc, 3 dc, sc) in each ch-3 sp around scallop. Break off.

Second scallop: work same as for first scallop until Row 8 is completed. Ch 1, turn. *Row 9:* Work (sc, 3 dc, sc) in each 3 ch-sp around scallop to within last 2 ch-3 sps, (in next sp work sc, dc, drop lp from hook, insert hook on right side in corresponding dc on preceding scallop, draw dropped lp through, work 2 more dc and sc in same sp on new scallop) 2 times. Break off. Continue making and joining scallops in this manner for 36 scallops.

Heading: *Row 1:* Working on the right side across straight edge of scallops, attach yarn with sl st to last sc in Row 9 of first scallop; ch 5, * sk ½ inch on horizontal edge, dc in edge, ch 2. Rep from * across, ending with ch 2, dc in last sc on ch 4, ch 3, turn. *Row 2:* Tr in first ch-2 sp, * ch 1, holding back last lp of each tr, work 2 tr over next ch-2 sp, yo and draw through all 3 lps on hook—tr-cluster made. Rep from * across, ending with tr-cluster over turning ch. Ch 1, turn. In each ch-1 sp make sc, dc, sc. Sl st in first sc; break off.

To finish: Steam-press. Lay fabric on table; pin border in place, using one scallop in corner. Trim fabric to fit. Whipstitch edges of fabric, repin border, and sew to fabric. Press.
continued

CROCHET ABBREVIATIONS

ch	chain
sc	single crochet
dc	double crochet
tr	triple crochet
sk	skip
sl	slip
st(s)	stitch(es)
sl st	slip stitch
lp(s)	loop(s)
sp	space
rep	repeat
yo	yarn over
*	repeat whatever follows * as indicated.

Wildflower Pillow and Crewel Throw *(continued)*

These multi-purpose patterns are designed for use on the embroidered pillow and throw pictured on page 36. By varying the size of the motifs, you can use them for many other embroideries as well. For example, work one or more motifs on a box in crewel wool or pearl cotton. Or use the motifs for machine embroidery or tambour work.

For directions for these techniques, refer to the Contents pages.

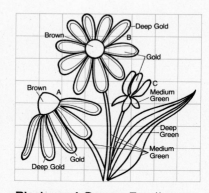

Black-eyed Susan: *For the embroidered pillow,* eliminate flower C. Petals of flowers A and B are double rows of gold chain stitches; centers are clusters of brown French knots; stems are couched and leaves are chain-stitched, both in medium green.

For the crewel throw, work as for the embroidered pillow.

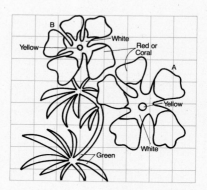

Gilia: *For the embroidered pillow,* use a single bloom of the Gilia (flower A), plus a spray of leaves. Work coral petals in satin stitches and white centers in fly stitches, with one yellow French knot at the center. Narrow leaves are single rows of blue-green chain stitches.

For the crewel throw, work the petals in coral satin stitches and outline stitches. In the centers, embroider a cluster of yellow French knots. Work the stem and leaves in forest green

wool, couching the stems with regular sewing thread. Work the leaves in rows of chain stitches.

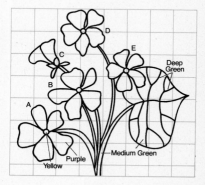

Violet: *For the embroidered pillow,* each petal is a single purple lazy daisy stitch filled with purple satin stitches; centers are yellow French knots; and stems are light green stem stitches. Work the leaf in light green satin stitches with darker green couched veins.

For the crewel throw, work petals in satin stitches. Flowers A, B, and D are deep purple; flowers C and E are medium purple. Centers are yellow French knots. Leaves are medium green satin stitches, with light green couched veins and stems.

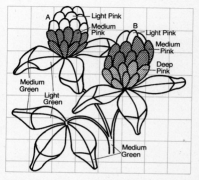

Clover: *For the embroidered pillow,* work both flowers in two shades of pink French knots.

Work stems in stem stitches and the leaves in fly stitches, both in medium green with random veins in darker green.

For the crewel throw, work flowers in two shades of pink French knots. Couch stems in grass green; leaves are grass-green satin stitches with veins of deeper green.

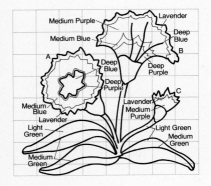

Bachelor's Button: *For the embroidered pillow,* work the flowers in medium blue long-and-short stitches with no shading. Embroider the stems in grass-green stem stitches and leaves in rows of chain stitches.

For the crewel throw, work flowers in purple long-and-short stitches, with flower centers in blue. Embroider base of each in green satin stitches; couch stems with regular thread; work leaves in split stitches.

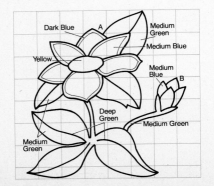

Hepatica: *For the embroidered pillow,* omit the bud (flower B), stems, and lower leaves. Work the petals of flower A in blue satin stitches; the center is pale yellow French knots; the leaves are closely worked rows of pale green satin stitches.

For the crewel throw, omit bud, stem, and lower leaves. Work petals and flower center as for embroidered pillow. Work leaves in green satin stitches.

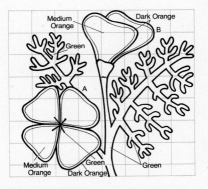

California Poppy: *For the embroidered pillow,* work petals in medium orange satin stitches, stems in green stem stitches, leaves in green fly stitches.

For the crewel throw, outline petals with dark orange stem stitches; work in light orange satin stitches. Work stem in grass-green couching and leaves in grass-green fly stitches.

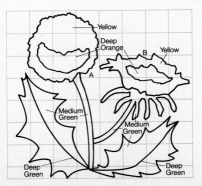

Dandelion: *For the embroidered pillow,* work all three flowers in medium yellow straight stitches (omit orange). Couch the stems in green, and embroider the leaves in tight rows of green chain stitches.

For the crewel throw, add the dandelion to the design, if you wish (it was not used in the afghan shown). Follow suggestions for the embroidered pillow, or work flowers in long-and-short stitches in yellow and dark orange yarn, as indicated on the pattern.

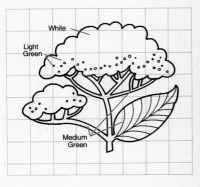

Queen Anne's Lace: *For the embroidered pillow,* work the stems in medium green chain stitches and the leaves in medium green leaf stitches. Embroider the flower heads in white French knots, or a combination of light green and white French knots or seed stitches.

For the crewel throw, add the Queen Anne's Lace design if you wish, following suggestions for the embroidered pillow.

Butterfly Album Cover

Butterflies are among nature's most beautiful creatures. Here, fanciful butterflies grace an album cover. Work this design using variations of just a few basic stitches.

Materials
20x36 inches off-white sailcloth
 or other closely woven fabric
9 skeins red embroidery floss
Tracing paper
16x14-inch purchased
 photograph album with
 removable covers
Spray adhesive
White glue
Paper for lining inside covers
Embroidery needle
Embroidery hoop or frame

Stitch Key
1 Stem stitch
2 Chain stitch
3 Knotted chain stitch
4 Double knot stitch
5 Cable chain stitch
6 French knot
7 Single feather stitch
8 Feather variation stitch
9 Satin stitch

Directions
Enlarge the butterfly design below, following directions on page 95. On an 18x20-inch piece of paper, center the album cover and trace around the outline. To make the pattern for the embroidery, trace a series of butterflies on the diagonal, referring to the photograph, if necessary. Use the outline of the album, which is marked on the paper, only as a guide for the placement of the butterflies. The 2-inch margin around the edges is for the extra fabric that will be turned under when the cover is assembled.

Transfer the design to the fabric, following directions on page 95. Note that you have just enough fabric to transfer the 18x20-inch design twice– for the front and back covers.

Mount the fabric in a hoop or frame and work the design, following the stitch guide. (See the Glossary on pages 90 to 93 for an explanation of the stitches.) Use 2 to 4 strands of embroidery floss, depending on the effect you want.

Block the completed embroidery by pressing the wrong side, using low heat. Pad the ironing board with a terry cloth towel to avoid crushing the raised portions of the design.

To attach the fabric to the photograph album, coat the front and back covers with fabric adhesive. Carefully stretch the fabric over the covers and pull the excess to the inside. Fold and clip the corners to reduce bulk, and secure edges with glue. To conceal the inside raw edges, cut two 13x13-inch pieces of paper and glue them to the inside of the album covers.

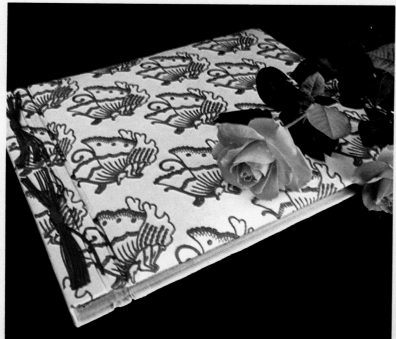

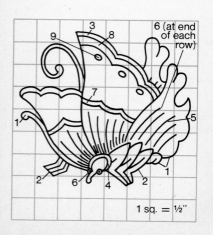

1 sq. = ½"

Crewel Embroidered Butterfly

Using only five different stitches, you can create this unique crewel design.

Materials

18x18 inches pale yellow linen or homespun fabric
1 small skein of Persian yarn in each of the following colors: rust, golden yellow, gold, pale gold, light orange, medium orange, burnt orange, butterscotch, pink, magenta, vermilion, and dark chartreuse
Embroidery needle
Tapestry needle
Four 14-inch wooden artist's stretcher strips
Staple gun or small tacks

Directions

Enlarge the butterfly design and transfer it to tracing paper. Center the design on the pressed fabric, leaving a 2-inch margin on each side, and transfer it, following directions on page 95.

Join the stretcher strips into a frame and stabilize the corners with staples. Stretch the fabric over the frame, centering the design, and staple the raw edges in back.

To work the design, follow the stitch and color keys for the pattern. Use a sharp embroidery needle for all the work *except* the spiderwebs; for these, use a blunt-end tapestry needle to avoid shredding the yarn as you weave. Use 2 or 3 strands of yarn, depending on the texture you prefer. (For an explanation of stitches, see the Glossary on pages 90 to 93.)

If the fabric is distorted when the embroidery is completed, remove it from the frame and press the wrong side with low heat. Then restretch the fabric over the frame, centering the design. Staple. Insert the butterfly picture in a purchased frame, if desired.

Color Key

A Rust
B Magenta
C Golden yellow
D Burnt orange
E Gold
F Pale gold
G Butterscotch
H Light orange
I Pink
J Dark chartreuse
K Vermilion
L Orange

Stitch Key

1 Chain stitch
2 Satin stitch
3 Split stitch
4 Stem stitch
5 Spiderweb stitch

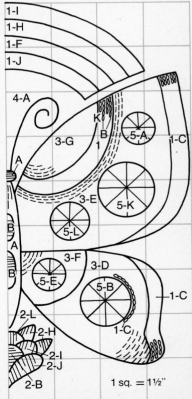

1 sq. = 1½"

A Walk in the Woods— Wall Hanging and Pillows

Take a stroll through a forest of crewel-embroidered trees and animals and learn many new stitches and techniques along the way.

Whether you are a beginner or a virtuoso with the needle, you can lavish all your creative skill on the sampler-like variety of stitches used in the 30x60-inch wall hanging shown above.

And if you are a saver, you may already have a

workbasket full of brown, green, blue, and gray threads to use in this stitchery. Forty-seven shades of floss and 20 shades of wool were used in the original hanging. But almost any combi- nation of earth-toned wools and cotton floss may be used effectively.

On the next four pages are patterns and stitch suggestions. Feel free to depart from them, though, and improvise in the placement and combination of stitches. Here is a chance to use your own creative impulses to make a stitchery that is uniquely your own.

continued

A Walk in the Woods—Wall Hanging and Pillows *(continued)*

1 sq.=1"

Materials

Wall Hanging

2 yards 36-inch-wide
   unbleached linen or linen-like
   fabric
Embroidery floss (see note)
3-ply crewel wool (see note)
Embroidery hoop (optional)

Embroidery needles
30x60-inch artist's stretcher
   strips or purchased frame

Pillows (shown on pages 34
and 35)

Two 22x22-inch pieces
   off-white linen or linen-like
   fabric for each pillow

Embroidery hoop
Embroidery needles
Blunt tapestry needles
DMC embroidery floss in the
   colors and amounts listed on
   page 47 or suitable substitutes
Pillow stuffing or 17-inch-square
   pillow forms

1 sq. = 1"

Directions
Wall Hanging

Note: If you wish to purchase yarn or floss, you will need gold, white, black, and ecru. You will also need varying shades—from pale to dark—in the following colors: yellow-green (olive), bronze green (khaki), blue-green (turquoise), blue, reddish-brown, golden brown, gray-brown, gray, orange-red, and yellow.

Enlarge the pattern above and transfer it to the fabric, leaving a 3-inch margin around the edges.

Embroider the design, using the photograph on pages 42 and 43 and these directions as guides.

Animals: All eyes are dark brown. Work in floss except as noted using 3, 4, or 5 strands.

continued

A Walk in the Woods—Wall Hanging and Pillows *(continued)*

Wall Hanging

Owl: Use two shades of beige for chest and face, brown wool for back feathers and face outline, gold for tail feathers and eyes, and white for accents. Work chiefly in long-and-short stitches; tail feathers are lazy daisy stitches; white accents are all open chain stitches.

Bunnies: For the pair, use light orange-red for one, light gold-beige for the other, with ecru accents on both. Work chiefly in long-and-short or twisted chain stitches, but use loose French knots for a fluffy tail. Work lettuce in dark olive wool buttonhole stitches. Work the single bunny in shades of ecru and light gold-beige twisted chain stitches. Noses are dark brown.

Bird: Use two shades of yellow, with a light turquoise neck ring and accents among the feathers. Beak is light brown. Work long-and-short stitches on head and body, leaf stitches on wings and tail, but make knotted chain stitches at tops of wings.

Squirrel: Use two shades of gray-brown, working head and body in long-and-short stitches, the tail in twisted chain stitches. Add loose French knots at top of tail. Outline in dark brown.

Ducks: Work heads and necks in medium and dark blue-green, with a yellow eye-band on one; feathers are shades of gray, turquoise, and dark green, with yellow and white accents. Beaks are gray, tipped in brown. Use long-and-short, twisted chain, leaf, and straight stitches.

Greenery: Use 1 strand of wool, except as noted. Work tree trunks in closely spaced rows of chain, buttonhole, or outline stitches in colors noted below.

For the large tree on the left, use dark gray and khaki green on the trunk. Work leaves in shades of olive and light yellow-green outline stitches. Work vine in gold-brown, with clusters of yellow French knots. For satin-stitched leaves, use two shades of blue-green floss.

For the large tree in the center, use medium and light gray, with accents in olive and black. Work mushrooms in medium reddish-brown; use satin stitches for caps, and chain stitches for stems.

For the large tree on the right, use light and medium gray-brown for trunk. Work wisps of vine in gold-brown outline stitches, and leaves in two shades of blue-green leaf stitches.

Work trunks of smaller trees in the background in brown and reddish-brown chain stitches. Leaves are yellow-green satin stitches, with stem-stitched outlines. Work round flowers at base of trees in two shades of brick-red buttonhole stitches, and leaves in two shades of olive outline and satin stitches.

Work wild strawberries (left) in brick-red wool and long-and-short stitches; outline with stem stitches. For leaves, use outline, feather, and straight stitches in shades of green.

Work pond background in shades of blue running stitches, ripples in blue outline stitches, and edge of water in blue straight stitches. Use brown outline stitches to define the edge of the pond and rocks on the shore.

Work reeds near bunnies in three shades of blue-green, using satin and leaf stitches.

Work large leaves on shore (right) in shades of olive and yellow-green wool, using chain, outline, long-and-short, and twisted chain stitches. Stems are dark brown and green outline stitches.

Work squirrel's branch in outline stitches in shades of brown, with leaves in olive and shades of blue-green satin stitches and long twisted chain stitches. Use dark brick-red wool for berries; pad first (directions are on page 24) and then satin-stitch.

Block the fabric following directions on page 78. Mount on stretcher strips.

Pillows

Enlarge the patterns opposite and transfer to fabric. Refer to the photograph on pages 34 and 35 for suggested distribution and combinations of colors.

Both pillows are relatively simple, and may be worked in any combination of traditional stitches using 2 to 6 strands of floss, depending on the effect desired. However, a more experienced embroiderer may want to experiment with some of the more adventuresome stitches described below.

On both pillows, tails of animals are worked in twisted chain stitches; the end of each is a series of twisted chain ring stitches (using 3 strands of floss) to give it a fluffy appearance.

Some fruit on pillow B is worked in velvet stitches; the rest is worked in spiderweb stitches, both using 6 strands of floss.

Many of the leaves on each pillow are executed in herringbone and fishbone leaf stitches (using 3 or 4 strands of floss).

Try padded satin stitches on the red berries on pillow A to add dimension (3 strands). Outline with chain stitches.

Use 4 strands of floss and a buttonhole picot stitch for the petals of the small coral flowers on the left side of pillow A.

Leaves of the plant at the base of the tree on pillow A may be worked with 3 strands in chain scroll stitches.

Whipped chain stitches (4 strands) are used for texture and dimension on the stem of the plant on the right of pillow B.

Cable chain stitches (4 strands) give an airy texture to the fringe of leaves on the same plant.

When the embroidery is finished, block the pillow top and press gently on the wrong side. Stitch top to backing fabric, turn, press, stuff, and slip-stitch.

DMC embroidery floss

No.　Skeins/Color

Pillow A

No.	Skeins	Color
225	1	Light rose
224	1	Medium rose
368	1	Light yellow-green
732	1	Dark yellow-green
780	1	Dark golden yellow
833	1	Light olive green
401	1	Light red-brown
613	1	Pale burnt umber
734	1	Light bronze green
421	1	Medium tan
3327	2	Dark red
936	2	Light avocado
935	2	Medium avocado
937	3	Medium-dark avocado
434	3	Warm brown
614	3	Light burnt umber
320	4	Medium yellow-green
801	5	Coffee brown

Pillow B

No.	Skeins	Color
225	1	Light rose
224	1	Medium rose
732	1	Dark yellow-green
580	1	Dark moss green
834	1	Pale olive
830	1	Dark olive
401	1	Light red-brown
3327	1	Dark red
368	2	Light yellow-green
833	2	Light olive
434	2	Warm brown
613	2	Pale burnt umber
936	2	Light avocado
935	2	Dark avocado
421	3	Medium tan
614	3	Light burnt umber
320	5	Medium yellow-green
937	5	Medium-dark avocado
801	5	Coffee brown

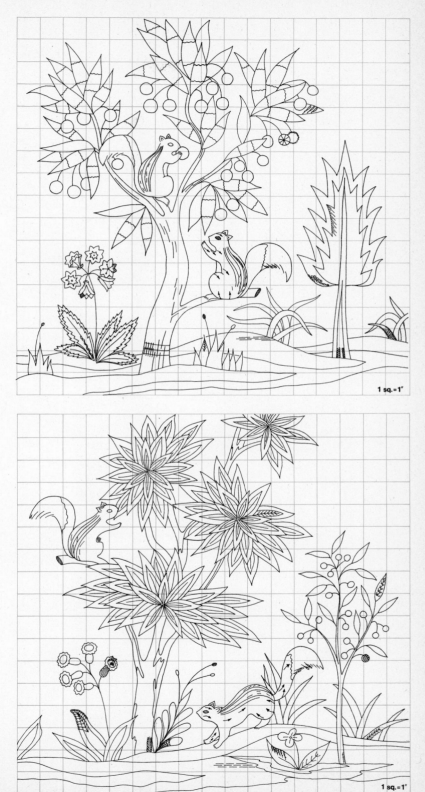

1 sq. = 1"

1 sq. = 1"

Cross-Stitch and Counted-Thread Techniques

In cross-stitch and counted-thread embroideries, each stitch is carefully sized and placed according to the number of strands in the fabric. The embroidery is developed by counting the number of threads in the material. The result is a beautifully embellished, precise, and well-scaled piece of needlework that is versatile enough to use in any number of ways.

To help get you started in this extremely popular embroidery technique, here is a whole section of cross-stitch and counted-thread project ideas, including pillowcases, towels, place mats, napkins, and a baby quilt. For how-to instructions for the dramatic and colorful table runner shown here, see page 64.

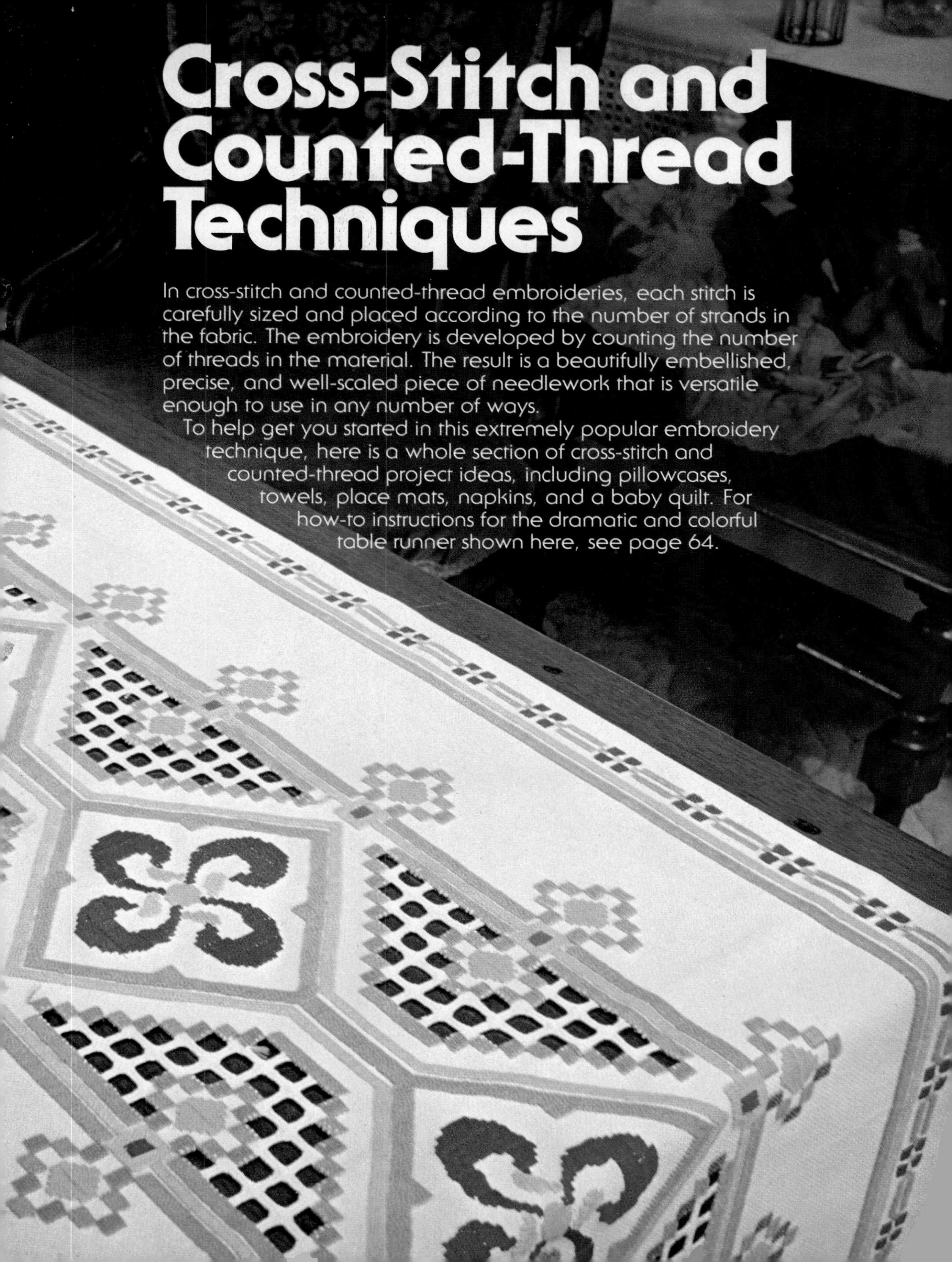

Auntie Dee's Cross-Stitch Tablecloth

This colorful tablecloth, worked entirely in cross-stitch, is an elaborate-looking design that is actually easy to embroider. The same motif adorns all four corners of the tablecloth, and the border pattern is composed of several simple designs. To further embellish your work, create your own cross-stitched initials for the center of the cloth.

Size your cloth according to our directions so the finished piece will fit your table.

Materials

Sufficient even-weave fabric for your tablecloth (see note below)

#3 pearl cotton in black, gold blue, avocado, and coral

Tapestry needle

Embroidery hoop (optional)

Graph paper (10 squares per inch)

Colored pencils to match thread

Directions

Note: This tablecloth can be worked on 68x68 inches of #18-count linen to be about 62 inches square when finished. If worked on 54x54 inches of #22-count Hardanger cloth, over 2 threads, it will be about 52 inches square when finished.

Using colored pencils, transfer the pattern to graph paper. Begin with the border shown in diagram A, then complete the square corner motif, one quarter of which is shown in diagram B. Note that the inside rows of stitches in the large square are the vertical and horizontal centers of the pattern; they are not part of the repeat.

Stay-stitch the edges of the fabric to prevent fraying. If desired, mount the fabric in a hoop to help prevent puckering.

Before you begin stitching, it is a good idea to make a few practice stitches to decide how many threads of the fabric you want to cover with each stitch. This tablecloth was embroidered with each stitch going over 2 threads of #18-count fabric. If your fabric has a different count, or if you would like a larger design, practice stitching over 3 or 4 threads to see which you prefer. Make a rectangular cloth with this design simply by shortening the border between the corner motifs. When doing this, though, plan the stitch pattern carefully on graph paper before embroidering.

Using a blunt tapestry needle for the embroidery, work pearl cotton through the spaces *between* the threads in the fabric. (Embroider the complete design in cross-stitches.)

Rather than tying knots on the back of your cloth, weave the ends of the threads into the back of the work, or begin and end with waste knots. (To make a waste knot, knot the end of the thread and insert the needle into the fabric from front to back so the knot is on top. Then stitch over the thread end, securing it. Clip the knot and pull the end to the back of the fabric.)

Allowing about a 4-inch margin of fabric around the edges, start the embroidery in one corner. Embroider the border corner first (diagram A). Work the repeat section of the border 20 more times, or as many times as you need for your cloth. Be sure to leave sufficient space at the next corner to work the corner border pattern again. Work the border completely around the cloth.

Work the square corner motifs, allowing ¾ inch between the top of the border and the edge of the corner square.

After the embroidery is completed, block the cloth and press it lightly. Allowing a margin of 4 threads below the coral swag in the border, withdraw 1 thread from the fabric completely around the cloth for hemstitching. Turn up a ⅝-inch hem and finish with hemstitching, following the directions on page 26.

Color Key
- 🕮 Coral
- ⊟ Blue
- ◩ Avocado
- ⊡ Gold
- ⊠ Black

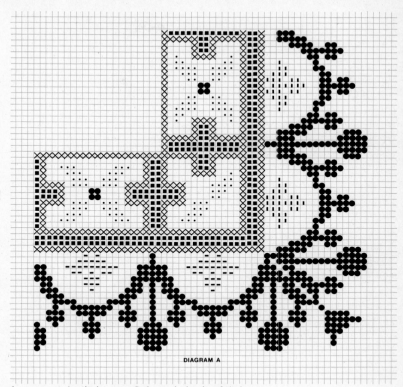

DIAGRAM A

1 square=1 stitch over 2 threads in the fabric

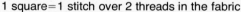

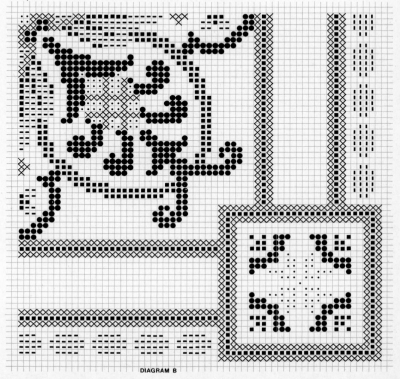

DIAGRAM B

Cross-Stitch Baby Quilt and Embroidered Pillow

To create a keepsake that can be proudly handed down generation after generation, embroider this delightful cross-stitch alphabet quilt. The crib-size quilt can be worked on your choice of fabrics, using any color embroidery floss, although red is traditional. To make your coverlet special, embroider the baby's name and birth date in one of the corners.

Materials

45x45 inches white #40-count even-weave fabric, #22-count Hardanger cloth, or fine percale for quilt top (see note below)

45x45 inches white fabric for quilt back

20x20 inches white fabric for pillow top (same as above)

Two 20x10½-inch pieces white fabric (pillow back)

½ yard muslin

Pillow stuffing

Red embroidery floss

Embroidery or tapestry needle (depending on fabric)

Quilt batting

Embroidery hoop (optional)

#14 mono-canvas (optional)

Directions

Note: If worked on #40-count fabric, the finished quilt will be about 38x38 inches. If worked on #22-count Hardanger cloth, it will be about 41x41 inches. Or, worked through #14 mono-canvas (waste canvas) on percale, it will be about 43 inches square. Depending on the fabric used, there will be similar variations in the size of the pillow top. We tell you how to use all three fabrics, so you can work with the one you prefer. Preshrink fabric and thread, if desired.

On #40-count cloth, use a tapestry needle; work each stitch over 5 threads of the fabric. On #22-count Hardanger, use a tapestry needle; work each stitch over 3 threads. On fine percale, use a sharp needle and baste #14 mono-canvas in place as a guide for stitch placement. Work the design over 2 threads of the canvas. After stitching, moisten the canvas, snip the threads, and gently withdraw each thread from beneath the stitches.

Mark the center of one side of the fabric 1 inch from the edge. Using the chart on pages 54 and 55, work the entire design; start in the center. Follow the placement diagram and stitch chart for the upper left corner to work borders and boxes for the letters, referring to the photograph if necessary. Then work letters shown on page 55, centering them in the boxes. Use 3 strands of floss.

Insert the fabric in a hoop or frame for working, if desired.

When you have finished embroidering the quilt top, outline-stitch the baby's name and date of birth in the lower right-hand corner. Finally, block the quilt top following directions on page 78.

To assemble the quilt, lay the backing on a flat surface. Smooth a 45-inch square of batting on top, and place the embroidered piece on top of that. Pin and baste the layers together.

Quilt with red floss, using one of the following methods: work cross-stitches in center of squares between letters, or cross-stitch over cross-stitches already completed. Or tie double strands of floss in center of squares between letters and clip ends to ½ inch. Or quilt with quilting thread in any traditional pattern. Remove basting threads after quilting is completed.

To bind the edges, trim batting and backing so they extend 1 inch beyond the outermost row of cross-stitches on the front of the quilt. Trim quilt top to ½ inch beyond the edge of backing and batting—1½ inches beyond the cross-stitched border. Turn under the raw edge of the top ¼ inch, fold top over batting and backing, and slip-stitch to the back of the quilt, mitering corners.

To make the pillow, embroider the design, following the diagram on page 54. After blocking, trim pillow top so raw edges fall 2½ inches outside the cross-stitched border. Use two pieces of white fabric to construct a layered back for the pillow, making it a sham. (Dimensions of the pillow front and back will depend on the fabric used for the embroidery.) Measure the completed cover; sew and stuff a muslin pillow to fit.

To care for the embroidered quilt, wash by hand or on the *gentle* cycle in a machine, using lukewarm water and mild soap or detergent. Do not wring out excess water; spin dry or roll in a towel to remove excess water, then dry the quilt flat. Be especially careful when washing to avoid hard machine action; it can pull the batting apart and make the quilt lumpy. If necessary, press the quilt while it is slightly damp, using a warm—not hot—iron.

continued

Cross-Stitch Baby Quilt and Embroidered Pillow *(continued)*

Stitch key
1 Cross-stitch
2 Outline stitch
3 Straight stitch
4 French knot
5 Lazy daisy (chain)

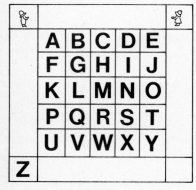

Upper right corner, quilt.

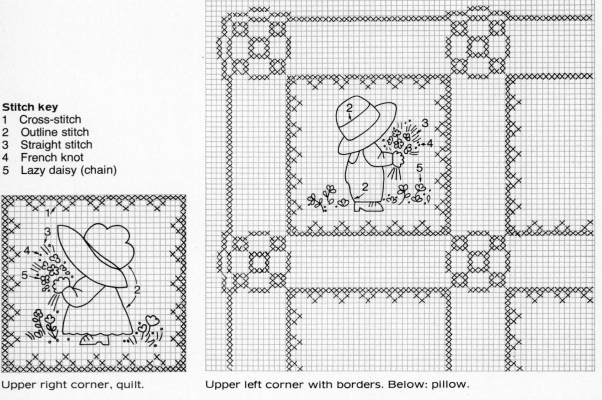

Upper left corner with borders. Below: pillow.

A	B	C	D	E
F	G	H	I	J
K	L	M	N	O
P	Q	R	S	T
U	V	W	X	Y
Z				

Placement diagram.

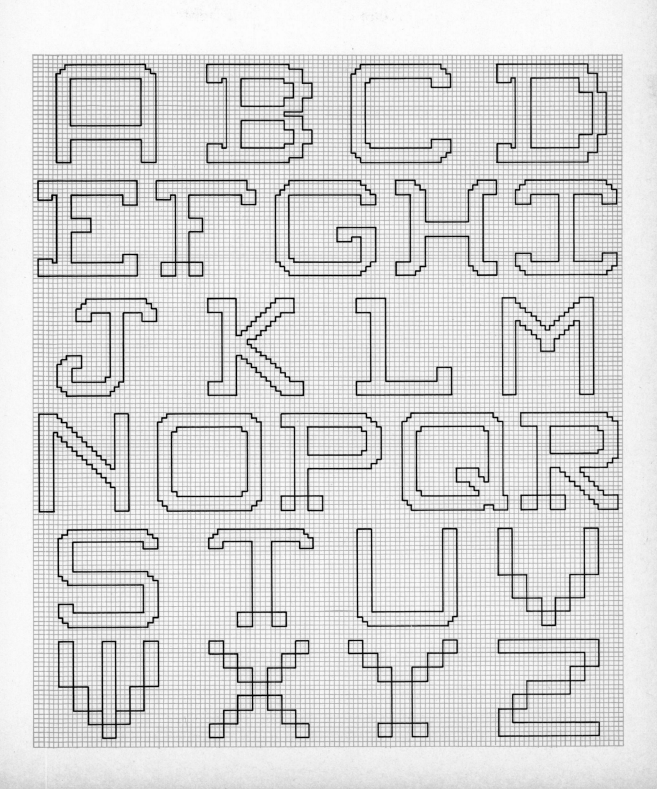

Cross-Stitch Pillowcases and Guest Towel

To adorn plain pillow-cases and hand towels, embroider these charming bird and flower motifs, worked primarily in cross-stitches. The easy-to-follow patterns will add delightful color accents to your linen collection.

Materials
Pillowcases
Pair of white pillowcases
Copen blue embroidery floss
Scraps of #12-count
  needlepoint mono-canvas
Embroidery needle
Embroidery hoop or frame
  (optional)
Guest Towel
14x27 inches white linen or
  huck toweling
Embroidery floss in the
  following colors: light
  blue-purple, dark blue-purple,
  green, yellow, orange, light
  pink, medium pink, dark pink,
  light lavender, dark lavender,
  purple, and reddish-purple
Embroidery hoop (optional)
Embroidery needle
Graph paper (10 squares per
  inch) (optional)
Colored pencils to match thread
  (optional)

Directions
Pillowcases: Baste the needlepoint canvas to the front of the pillow-case directly above the stitching line for the hem. Use the mesh in the canvas as a guide for the placement of stitches. Mount the fabric in a hoop, if desired. Starting in the lower center of the chart, work the design entirely in cross-stitches. Use 2 strands of floss throughout, and work each stitch over 2 threads of canvas.

When the embroidery is finished, dampen the canvas, snip the threads, and remove them from beneath the stitches. If desired, re-move the hem and re-hem with a line of decorative hemstitching.

Guest Towel: If you are working with linen, turn under a narrow hem on the long sides. For linen and huck toweling, turn up a 1-inch hem at each end and hemstitch, following directions on page 26.

Find the center of one short end of the fabric and the center of the design and begin working there. Work the light blue-purple outline in cross-stitches 1 inch above the hemstitching. Then work the dark blue-purple outline, following the graph.

Work flowers and leaves according to the chart. All work is done in cross-stitches *except* the green outline and lazy daisy stitches for the stems and leaves, and the French knot flowers.

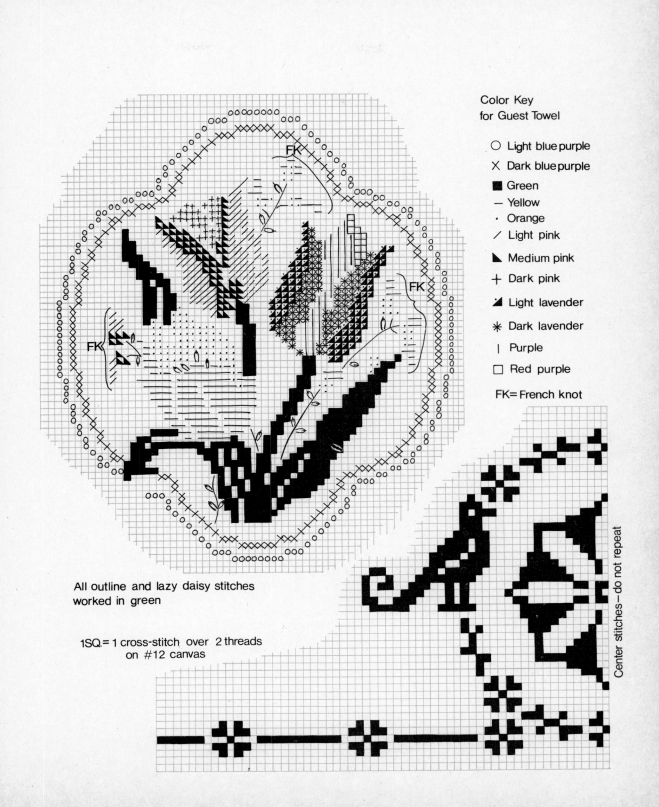

Color Key
for Guest Towel

○ Light blue purple
✕ Dark blue purple
■ Green
— Yellow
· Orange
╱ Light pink
◣ Medium pink
+ Dark pink
◢ Light lavender
✳ Dark lavender
| Purple
□ Red purple

FK= French knot

All outline and lazy daisy stitches
worked in green

1 SQ. = 1 cross-stitch over 2 threads
on #12 canvas

Center stitches — do not repeat

Hardanger Place Mat and Napkin

*The table accessories
shown here are stitched in
a traditional counted-
thread technique from
the Hardanger province
of Norway. Worked
on even-weave fabric, the
design is embroidered
in blocks of satin stitches
and accented with
cutwork and delicate
needleweaving.*

*We think you will enjoy
this challenging and
elegant addition to your
needlework repertoire.*

Materials
17x12 inches #22-count white
   Hardanger cloth (for each
   place mat)
16x16 inches #22-count white
   Hardanger cloth (for each
   napkin)
White #5 pearl cotton
White #8 pearl cotton, lace or
   crochet thread
Graph paper (10 squares per
   inch)
Small, sharp-pointed scissors
Tapestry needles (small)

Directions
The diagram on page 60 is for a portion of the pattern on the place mat, showing part of the corner and side. Transfer it to graph paper, using a large enough piece (or several pieces taped together) so that there are the same number of spaces and lines on the paper as spaces and threads on the place mat. In that way, you can see the exact location of each stitch and be sure that stitches are accurately placed in relation to the total design.

The repeat for the sides of the place mat is marked on the diagram. To complete the pattern, turn the repeat area over so the "A" sides match. When working the corner, reverse the pattern and match it along the diagonal, as indicated.

After working the place mat, graph the design for the napkin by referring to the photograph. Or work a segment of the same pattern embroidered on the place mat.

Before doing any cutwork, embroider the satin stitches using #5 pearl cotton. While stitching, be careful to work the thread through the *spaces* between the threads rather than into the threads themselves. Work blocks of 5 stitches over 4 threads of the fabric — always working one more stitch than the number of threads to be cut, so the cut area is sufficiently bound and will not ravel. Cut areas *must* be edged with satin-stitched blocks.

Work stitches in the sequence shown in diagram A on page 60. When 2 stitches share a space in a corner, bring the thread up through the same space on the inside corner of each block.

When all the satin stitching is finished, do the cutwork. Cut only those threads that are bound with satin-stitched blocks — and indicated on the pattern diagram. Use small, sharp-pointed scissors and cut close to the satin stitching. (The fabric will shrink when washed, and frayed edges will not show.) Cut both ends of block-bound threads and gently lift the cut threads from the fabric with a needle. The fabric will look like diagram B on page 60.

Next, thread a smaller needle with #8 pearl cotton or lace or crochet thread, and anchor the end of the thread under the satin stitching. Bring it up in the center of the threads to be woven — indicated with an "X" on diagram B. Go over 2 threads on the left, wrapping thread around them, and bring the needle up again in the center. Next, go over 2 threads on the right. Continue, pulling threads tightly together as you weave and maintaining even tension.

At the end of a woven area, turn the corner and weave the adjoining threads, always starting with the needle in the *center* of the two pairs of threads. If woven threads are distorted at the end of a block, you have woven too many or too few times over the threads. Make necessary adjustments and continue. Do not end or start a thread in the middle of a row of weaving.

Plan the stitching to weave threads that form a square in either a clockwise or counterclockwise direction. Then, when making the tiny loops joining the pairs of woven threads, work in the opposite direction. To make the loops, weave three sides of the square and half of the fourth. Then make the loops as shown in diagram C on page 60, working the thread through the *center* of the needle-woven pairs, rather than around them. Work one loop on each side of the square, and then finish weaving the fourth side.

When the embroidery is finished, turn up a narrow (¼-inch) hem.

continued

Hardanger Place Mat and Napkin *(continued)*

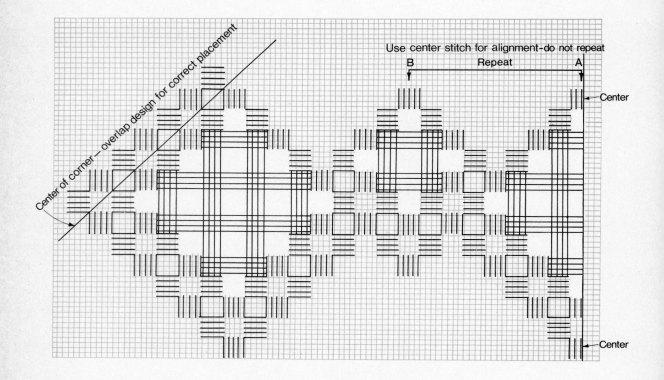

Center of corner — overlap design for correct placement

Use center stitch for alignment-do not repeat

B — Repeat — A

Center

Center

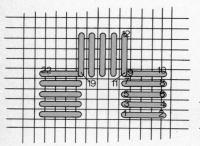

DIAGRAM A
Making satin-stitched blocks

DIAGRAM B
Needleweaving in cut areas

Needle-Weaving

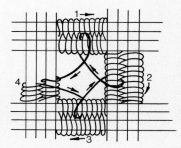

DIAGRAM C
Working the loops

Blackwork Embroidery Scroll

Directions

Enlarge the pattern on the next page and transfer it to fabric.

Work the design by filling numbered areas with stitch patterns shown on pages 62 and 63. Use the number of strands indicated in the chart. Varying the number of strands and the density of the patterns creates shading in the design.

To fill an area, begin in the center and work complete stitch patterns toward the edges. At the edges, work only a portion of the stitch pattern, if necessary. After filling, outline-stitch each shape using 2 strands of floss along the denser side of each pattern and 1 strand along the lighter side. Work the man in outline stitches. Use straight stitches for pine needles and grass.

Block the finished embroidery and stitch it to the satin backing fabric, leaving an opening for turning. Clip corners, turn, and press. Tack to dowels that have been cut to size and painted black. Add black beads at ends of dowels.

continued

Subtle shading is the key to this handsome blackwork embroidery piece, worked on white linen and accented with black details. The stitches are carefully counted and placed so that they gradually fade from dark to light.

Materials

7x10 inches #30-count even-weave linen, or 10x13 inches #18- or #22-count even-weave fabric (see note on page 62)
Black embroidery floss
Tapestry needle
10x13 inches white satin
16 inches of ¼-inch-diameter dowel
4 beads with ¼-inch holes
Black paint

Blackwork Embroidery Scroll *(continued)*

The stitch designs below are fillings to use in the embroidered scroll. Numbers and shading (dark, medium, and light) correspond to numbers and shading on the diagram at left. Use the number of strands of floss indicated on the shading chart, opposite. Embroider the patterns in backstitches, double running stitches, and running or darning stitches, working each stitch over the number of threads indicated by the lines on the chart.

1 SQ.=1 IN.

For #30-count fabric, enlarge the pattern to a scale of "one square equals one inch;" for #18- or #22-count fabric the scale is "one square equals 1½ inches."

The finished size of the scroll on #30-count fabric is 5x7 inches; on other fabrics, it is about 8x11 inches.

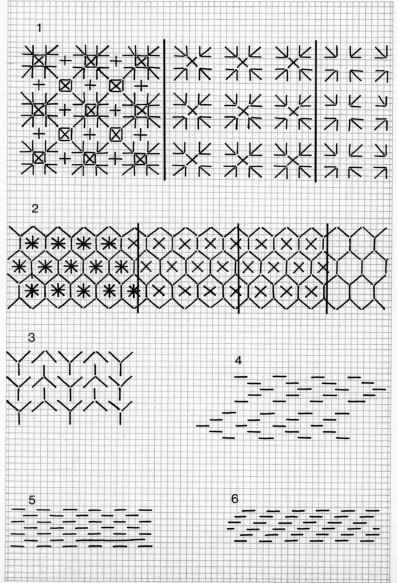

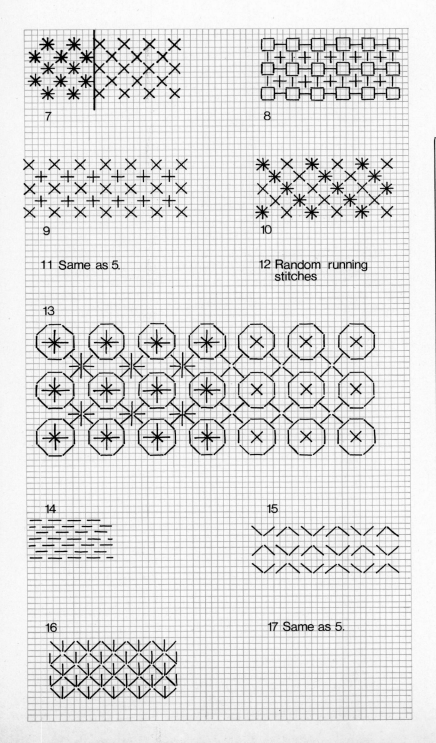

7

8

9

10

11 Same as 5.

12 Random running stitches

13

14

15

16

17 Same as 5.

SHADING CHART

Pattern	Shade	Strands
1	Dark	2
	Medium	2
	Light	1
2	Dark	2
	Medium	2
	Medium	1
	Light	1
3		1
4		1
5		1
6		1
7	Dark	1
	Medium	1
8		1
9		1
10		1
13		1
14		1
15		1
16		1

Auntie Dee's Embroidered Runner

(shown on pages 48 and 49)

An interesting combination of cutwork, needle weaving, and embroidery makes this table runner truly unique. The satin stitching and other details are exquisite, whether seen close up or from far away.

Materials
24x72 inches of #22-count Hardanger cloth
#5 pearl cotton in scarlet, medium blue, light green, and yellow
#8 pearl cotton in white, or white lace thread
Large sheets of graph paper (10 squares per inch)
Colored pencils to match thread
Embroidery hoop or frame
Small tapestry needles
Small, sharp scissors

Color Key
S   Scarlet
B   Blue
G   Green
Y   Yellow

Directions
Use colored pencils and graph paper to make a drawing of the pattern at right. Note that it is for one quarter of the motif only. Transfer it to paper and complete the pattern for the central swirl motif inside the diamond and the cutwork borders separately.

Make the diamond motif, including the central swirl, by lining up side B next to side A, and transferring the design. Continue in this "circular" fashion until the swirl is complete. For the borders and cutwork, reverse the pattern and match the C sides. Then reverse the pattern again on the D side, matching along the center, and complete the upper half.

Begin stitching in the center of the cloth, stretching the fabric in a hoop or frame to prevent puckering. Work the design first in straight stitches over the number of threads indicated. Work from the center of the fabric across the width, omitting the continuous blue line of satin stitches in the lower border at this stage.

After working the motif across the fabric, work the design the length of the runner. Be sure you leave enough fabric at the ends to work the lower border around the corners and across the ends.

Work the design in colored threads before starting the cutwork. For the cutwork, carefully cut away the threads that are missing in the diagram, leaving those that appear as dark lines. Use sharp scissors and work in good light. Then work needle weaving over the threads remaining between colored areas. (See page 58 for specific directions for this Hardanger cutwork.)

When the entire pattern (including the cutwork) is finished, turn up the hem 13 threads below the scarlet blocks and whipstitch in place. Then work the blue line over 5 threads of the fabric and completely around the cloth, catching in the hem margin at the same time. Block the fabric, following instructions on page 78.

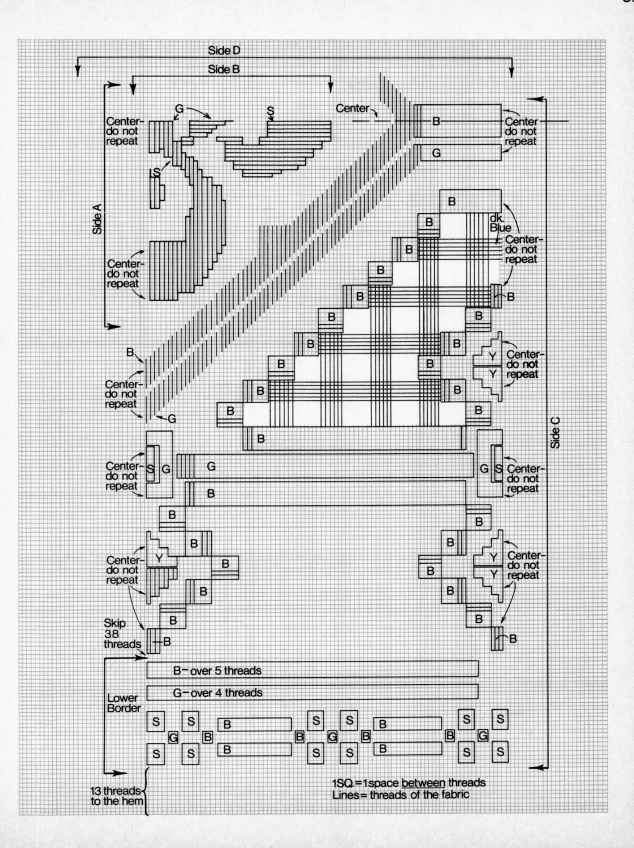

Side D

Side B

G S Center

Center-do not repeat

B Center-do not repeat

G

Side A

I S

B dk. Blue Center-do not repeat

B

B B

B

Center-do not repeat

B B

B Y Center-do not repeat
Y

B

B B

B

B B

B B

B B

B

B

Center-do not repeat

G

S G G G S Center-do not repeat

Center-do not repeat B

B B

B B

Center-do not repeat Y B B Y Center-do not repeat
B B

B B

Skip 38 threads B B

B— over 5 threads

G— over 4 threads

Lower Border

S S B S S B S S

G B B G B G

S S B S S B S S

Side C

13 threads to the hem

1 SQ. = 1 space between threads
Lines = threads of the fabric

Machine Embroidery

Whatever its make or model, your home sewing machine can stitch up a lot more than an occasional seam. For something new in embroidery, we suggest you try creative machine stitchery to make lovely and exciting accessories for your home. In this section, we have included projects ranging from simple crazy-quilt machine embroidery to the more challenging free-motion work shown in the curtains and pillowcase below. For how-to information, see page 74.

Machine Embroidery Basics

If you have access to a sewing machine, you can do machine stitchery and enjoy all sorts of embroidered projects that you might not have time to work by hand. And while we won't deny that practice makes perfect, embroidering on your sewing machine is not difficult once you understand the basics of this kind of needlework.

On these two pages, you will learn some of the basics of machine stitchery that will guide you to successful completion of the projects that follow.

Fabrics

Any fabric can serve as a ground for machine embroidery, although some are easier to stitch on than others. Medium-weight, firmly woven fabrics in particular, such as denim or sailcloth, are easiest to learn on.

Lightweight fabrics, such as broadcloth and sheers, tend to pucker under the needle. Strengthen and stabilize them by backing them with a sheet of typing paper (be sure to pull it away after stitching). If you use iron-on interfacing, test a scrap of fabric with the interfacing before applying it—to be sure the adhesive does not mar the face fabric.

Also back medium-weight fabrics that need extra support with iron-on interfacing or typing paper.

Nubby and napped fabrics, such as terry cloth or velvet, do not take a pattern easily and can be hard to stitch. Solve these problems by drawing the pattern on tissue paper and basting or pinning it to the face of the fabric before inserting it into an embroidery hoop. Stabilize the fabric further with a layer of tissue or typing paper on the back (after stitching, remove paper).

When stitching heavy fabrics, such as upholstery-weight materials, or fabrics with naps that crush easily, do not use an embroidery hoop. Instead, keep the fabric taut with your fingers. Use the thumb and index fingers of each hand to hold fabric and feed it under the needle.

To embroider on knits and other fabrics that stretch, stabilize the back of the fabric with muslin or iron-on interfacing.

Threads

Any thread can be used for machine stitchery, although 100 percent cotton thread is preferable for most projects. Try cotton machine embroidery thread, using a larger thread (such as size 30) on the spool and a smaller thread (size 50) in the bobbin. For most projects, use white thread in the bobbin regardless of the color of the top thread—it will not show.

The heavier thread on the spool has a rich texture and fills the design faster than more slender thread. At the same time the smaller thread in the bobbin eliminates some of the bulk on the back of the fabric for a neater and more even finish.

Rayon, silk, and metallic machine embroidery threads are worth trying for their special effects. When buying metallic thread, though, be sure to choose thread that is smooth enough to feed evenly through the needle.

For some types of machine stitchery, transparent nylon thread is best. With it, you can invisibly couch yarns to fabric (for crewel work on the sewing machine). It is also useful for couching thick threads (including metallics) that cannot be stitched in the needle.

Equipment

Sharp sewing machine needles are a must for machine embroidery. Keep a supply of needles in various sizes on hand and change them often, using a new needle for every project.

For most machine stitchery, use an embroidery hoop to keep the fabric drum-tight under the needle. A round or oval hoop with a tension screw works well. It must be small enough in diameter to move under the needle without bumping the side of the machine. Wrap the inner ring with twill or bias tape to help keep the fabric taut.

Mount the fabric in the hoop upside down—so it will lie flat on the bed of the sewing machine with the design facing up.

Tighten the tension screw to hold the fabric firmly.

There is also an embroidery hoop available that is especially nice for machine work on light and medium-weight fabrics. The inner ring pops into a U-shaped channel in the outer ring.

Adjusting the Machine

Check your machine to see that it is in good working order before you begin. In particular, see that it is well-oiled, for embroidery requires more frequent lubrication of your machine than regular home sewing. Also, clean accumulated lint from the machine often—especially the bobbin case.

Adjust the tension on the spool and the bobbin, if necessary. You may need to loosen the top tension slightly. To check tension adjustment, lower the presser bar and work some practice stitches on a piece of scrap fabric. Then check the position of the spool and bobbin threads on both sides of the material. The top thread should pull slightly to the underside of the fabric and the bobbin thread should not be visible on the face of the fabric.

Before stitching, check tension with a sample of the fabric to be embroidered to be sure the material does not pucker. If it does, loosen the tension.

Always lower the presser bar to engage the tension on the upper thread when you stitch, even for free-motion embroidery when there is no presser foot in place. Otherwise, thread does not feed properly through the machine and bobbin thread will pile up on the back of the fabric.

For free-motion embroidery, lower or cover the feed dogs under the needle and remove the presser foot. Set the stitch length at zero or fine, and the width on zigzag machines anywhere from narrow to wide, depending on the effect you are striving for.

For more on free-motion work, see page 74.

Working the Stitches

Once you have checked your machine and mounted your fabric firmly in an embroidery hoop, you are ready to begin creative machine stitchery. There are several kinds of embroidery that you may wish to try before you experiment with free-motion.

If you have decorative cams or stitches on your machine, use them in your embroidery. Our crazy-quilt place mats on the following page are an example of this kind of embroidery.

You also can make attractive and decorative border designs using the fancy stitches on the machine. Simply combine the patterns, working them in complementary colors. See the diagrams at right for suggestions. Use an embroidery, darning, or other lightweight presser foot.

Decorative machine satin stitching makes an attractive edge on appliqué work. For this technique, first stitch the appliqué in place with medium-width, medium-length (10 to 12 stitches per inch) zigzag stitches. Trim excess beyond stitching.

Reset the machine for a wide but closely spaced, fine zigzag stitch (a machine satin stitch) and re-sew around the edges of the appliqué, machine-embroidering it in place. This is one of the techniques used on the tulip wall panel shown on page 72.

You may also wish to try free-motion embroidery using only straight stitches. For this technique, lower or cover feed dogs, remove the presser foot, and set stitch length at zero. Position the fabric under the needle, run the machine at a fairly fast speed, and "draw" with your needle—outlining and filling designs with straight stitches.

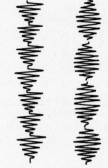

Decorative stitches

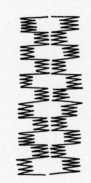

Using one pattern for a border

Combining patterns in a border

Crazy-Quilt Patchwork Place Mats

These crazy-quilt place mats are machine-embroidered the easiest way — by using the decorative stitches or cams on your sewing machine to anchor colorful scraps to background fabric.

Materials

Scraps of cotton fabrics
¾ yard 36-inch-wide fusible interfacing (for 2 place mats)
1 yard solid-color backing fabric
Contrasting bias binding
Steam iron
Embroidery thread in colors to complement fabrics

Directions

Pre-shrink all cotton fabrics, including the backing fabric. Cut two 13x16-inch ovals from the fusible interfacing and two from the backing material.

Cut interesting shapes from cotton scraps in complementary colors and prints, referring to the photograph for ideas, if necessary. Place them wrong side down on the adhesive side of the fusible interfacing. Overlap the edges slightly. Press with an iron until the scraps adhere to the interfacing.

Set your sewing machine on one of its decorative settings, or insert a decorative cam. Using a contrasting thread color, stitch around each fabric scrap to conceal the raw edges. Combine several decorative stitches, if you wish, or use double needles threaded with same- or different-colored threads.

Place right sides of the place mat's front and back together. Sew a ½-inch seam around raw edge, leaving room for turning. Clip curves, trim seams, and turn right side out. Slip-stitch openings closed. Baste bias binding over raw edges and stitch.

Machine-Embroidered Hardanger Place Mats

The simple beauty of machine stitchery is well-illustrated by these lovely place mats. Make them by bar-tacking—zigzag stitching back and forth across four threads of fabric, letting the embroidery thread build up on the fabric.

Even-weave fabrics are best for this technique, since their visible, interlocking threads act as a bar tacking guide as you stitch.

Materials

1⅛ yards of 42-inch-wide Hardanger cloth or other even-weave fabric (for 2 place mats and 2 napkins)
Light blue and dark blue embroidery thread
8-inch-diameter screw-type embroidery hoop
Tissue paper

Directions

Cut two pieces of fabric 16x13 inches for the place mats and two pieces 14x14 inches for the napkins. Set the machine for a wide zigzag stitch, and use dark blue thread on top and white thread in the bobbin. Lower the feed dogs and remove the presser foot.

Wrap inner hoop with bias tape to minimize creasing. Back place mats with tissue to prevent puckering, and clamp fabric in hoop right side up, with paper on the bottom (see photograph at right).

Referring to the photograph above for placement suggestions, follow the diagram at right to form bar-tacked squares and chevrons. Each zigzag stitch should cross 4 threads of the fabric.

Lower needle into fabric, and bring up bobbin thread. Bar-tack across 4 threads, repeating 5 times so threads build up on surface. Stitch 5 bar tacks side by side to form 1 side of the square.

With needle in top of fifth bar tack, pivot hoop so next series of bar tacks is perpendicular to first. Continue stitching and pivoting until there are 4 sets of 5 bar tacks around a common square. When finished, set stitch width to "0" and sew several stitches along side of bar tack to keep it from raveling.

Position needle for next set of bar tacks—about ¼ inch from first set—without cutting thread between bar-tacked squares.

When bar-tacked squares and light blue chevrons are completed, remove fabric from hoop. Sew a satin-stitched border 1 inch from raw edges and fringe, as shown. Trim all thread ends.

For napkins, satin-stitch a dark blue border ½ inch from the edge, with a second border ¼ inch inside the first. Add a light blue chevron in each corner. Trim fabric close to first border.

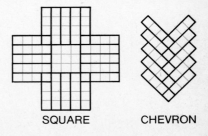

SQUARE   CHEVRON

Machine-Embroidered Wall Hanging

Tulips are in full bloom on this cheerful wall hanging, made with a variety of techniques, including machine embroidery, appliqué, and quilting. The stuffed nylon bulbs add dimension.

Materials

14x20 inches light blue fabric
10x20 inches brown, medium-weight drapery fabric
6x20 inches tulip-red velvet
Embroidery thread in the following colors: light, medium, and dark green, dark red, red to match velvet, yellow, medium brown, and black
12x14½ inches muslin
6-inch and 10-inch narrow embroidery hoops
1 pair medium-brown nylon stockings
Scraps of polyester fiberfill
Two 1x14-inch strips of wood lath
2 brass decorative screw eyes

Color Key
A   Dark Green
B   Medium green
C   Light green
D   Red
E   Dark red
F   Yellow
G   Medium brown
H   Black

Directions

Lap brown fabric ¾ inch over blue. Set machine for longest stitch and widest bight and sew pieces together with 10 rows of zigzag stitches in three shades of green, overlapping rows to form a band of grass 1 inch wide.

Enlarge pattern onto tissue paper, center it on fabric, and pin and machine-baste outlines of the design. Tear away tissue paper.

Mount fabric in hoop. Using light presser foot, work stems first in medium-wide satin stitches. Refer to tips for free-motion work on page 74, and begin center tulip. Work leaves in rows of wide satin stitches, reducing stitch width as width of leaf decreases and to accent leaf tips. Accent center veins with narrow zigzag stitches.

Make a bulb shape about ¾ inch thick by wrapping stocking around stuffing. Allow some stocking to double over, creating dark and light areas. Pin to background, folding and pleating to form pointed tops of bulbs. Sew down with narrow zigzag stitches. Stitch edges with a second row of medium-wide satin stitches, accenting pointed tips and widening stitches at the base. For inner contours, quilt the fabric with narrow zigzag stitches through all layers.

Embroider roots with narrow black satin stitches. Cut tulip appliqués ½ inch larger than pattern. Pin in place, and mount fabric in embroidery hoop on *wrong* side. Zigzag outlines and inner contours with matching thread. Trim excess velvet on front. Reinsert fabric in hoop. Satin-stitch around petals, varying width of stitch from wide (bulbous curves) to narrow (points). Use narrow zigzag for veins and yellow accents; work stamen in black.

To finish, cut fabric to 18x18 inches. Stitch muslin to sides, right sides together. Turn, press, and turn under ⅛ inch on top and bottom. Turn up 2-inch hem; blindstitch in place. Insert lath through casing at top and hang, or sew curtain rings to corners for hanging.

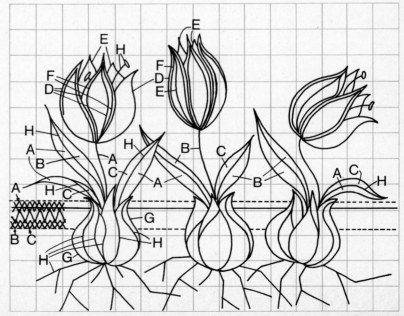

1SQ.=1IN.

Machine-Embroidered Curtains and Pillowcase

(shown on pages 66 and 67)

The embroidery on the curtains and pillowcase on pages 66 and 67 are examples of free-motion work on a sewing machine. For this technique, you work without a presser foot, but lower the presser bar to establish tension. Directions here include how-to for the projects shown, plus helpful free-motion stitchery tips.

Materials
Purchased pair of ready-made curtains or draperies
Machine embroidery thread in green, red, yellow, and white
Embroidery hoop
Pillowcase

For a Fine Finish—
Free-Motion Machine Embroidery

Whether you have a straight-stitch or a zigzag sewing machine, you can do free-motion embroidery. For with either machine, once you lower the feed dogs and remove the presser foot, you are free to move the fabric under the needle in any direction and to draw and stitch creatively with your needle. But, because the position of the sewing machine needle is stationary, the position of the design to be embroidered and the way you move the hoop beneath the needle are important for attractive machine stitchery.

A good guide to get you started is to position and then move the embroidery hoop so the stitches cover the fabric in much the same direction as they would in hand embroidery. For example, to hand-embroider a stem in satin stitches, you would work slightly slanted stitches down the length of the stem. For machine work, then, turn the design slightly at an angle as you slide the hoop under the needle. For a fine line—comparable to outline-stitching by hand—work with the design sideways under the needle.

To fill a shape by hand, you might use long-and-short stitches. For example, in the leaf below at left, hand-embroidered stitches would extend upward from the vein to the outer edge. For machine work, turn the design in the hoop sideways so the machine stitches will fall in the same direction (see diagram below).

When filling shapes, first outline the edges with narrow zigzag stitches. Then cover the inside of the shape with rows of wider zigzag stitches, as shown in the leaf diagram, opposite.

If a shape can be divided, embroider small sections individually—just as in hand embroidery. For example, work the petals of a flower separately. Stitch the top of a leaf first, then the lower half—dividing the shape along the vein (see leaf diagram, opposite). Or divide a star into diamond-shaped sections and stitch.

Always work filling stitches in the same direction as outline stitches. Also, do not rotate or swing the hoop as you stitch; move it back and forth, from side to side.

Moving the hoop back and forth evenly takes some practice. To get used to it, draw a curved line on fabric, mount it in a hoop, and embroider the line without turning the hoop. Or write your name and embroider it—without rotating the hoop.

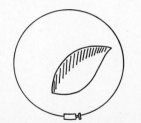

Mark direction of the stitches.

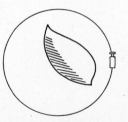

Turn the hoop sideways.

Directions

To embroider the curtains, first remove the hems. Make an iron-on transfer of the pattern below on tissue paper by tracing the design as many times as necessary to cover the width of the curtain. Then iron the pattern onto the curtain, positioning the lowest point in the design 1 inch from the hem fold.

Mount the fabric in a hoop; it must be taut. Place the design area under the needle sideways and work the stem in green thread. Do not rotate the hoop as you stitch—instead, move it back and forth. Work small buds in yellow thread.

With red thread, work the center section of the tulip first. Slide the hoop beneath the needle with the design turned sideways so the stitches fall vertically in the petal, as in the top diagram at right. Work side petals at an angle of about 45 degrees to the center, as shown in the top diagram at right. Finish by working a small circle at the base of the tulip to connect the side petals.

Clip all the threads close to the fabric and press the work into a terry cloth towel or other padded surface.

Replace the hem in the curtain by blindstitching by hand.

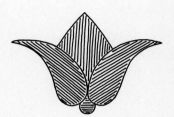

Stitch sections individually.

Outline and fill in the same direction.

For the pillowcase, use the pattern opposite. Machine-embroider the design following instructions above. The same pattern may be used along the top of a sheet for a matched set of linens.

Special Stitchery Techniques

After mastering basic embroidery techniques, it is time to try something new and different. In this section, we go beyond conventional projects and introduce an entirely new repertoire of stitches and ideas. Shisha mirrors, metal threads, and tambour work are only the beginning—the possibilities are endless. Adapt the projects to fit your needs and the materials available to you. And stay flexible enough to incorporate your own ideas into the patterns and stitchery suggestions given here.

Special embroidery techniques are not necessarily more difficult. They simply allow more creativity—and that is what embroidery is all about. For instructions for this richly embroidered shisha fish, please turn to page 87.

Metal Thread Work—Embroidered Panel

To add some sparkle to your stitchery, work with metal threads. While several kinds of silver can be used for embroidery, the stitchery panel shown opposite is worked in a twisted thread that is widely available at a modest price. Small beads and white floss add to the design.

If you have not worked in metal threads before, we think you will find this small project easy and fun to stitch.

Materials
9x15 inches green fabric
3-ply silver thread
1-ply silver thread
White embroidery floss
Black embroidery floss
Embroidery needles
6½x12-inch piece of cardboard
Twelve ⅛-inch-diameter
   transparent beads
Seventy ¹⁄₁₆-inch-diameter pearly
   beads

Directions
Enlarge the pattern and transfer it, centered, to the fabric following directions on page 95. Work the design in metallic threads and floss according to the color and stitch keys. Numbers in parentheses indicate the number of strands of thread to use.

Mount the finished embroidery on a piece of cardboard, following the directions below. Frame, if desired.

For A Fine Finish—Blocking and Mounting
Blocking and mounting are simple finishing procedures that add much to your embroidery. If your fabric has pulled out of shape while being stitched, straighten it by blocking. Then, if it is a piece that requires mounting, finish it for hanging.

Stitchery worked in a hoop or frame should not need much blocking. Remove it from the frame and steam-press it gently (on low heat) on the wrong side over a thickly padded ironing board. Pin it to the board to hold it in place, if necessary, and use a damp cloth between the fabric and the iron. If colors might run, insert a dry cloth between the stitchery and the damp cloth.

If you have worked the embroidery in your lap, block it on a board with pins, tacks, or staples. Use cork or insulation board and T-pins (used for macrame) or plywood and thumbtacks or staples. Pad the board first with soft toweling. Use 1-inch checked gingham for the top layer of padding—it is an easy reference for straightening the grain of the fabric and sizing the embroidery.

Pin or staple the padding to the board. Lay the embroidery over the padding, face down, and secure it in the *center* of each side. Then gently stretch it and secure it to the board, working from the center toward the corners. Insert pins or staples into the margins of the fabric only. Keep grain lines straight and fabric taut. Finally, dampen the fabric and let it dry thoroughly.

If the piece is to be mounted and it ravels easily, stay-stitch the edges by hand or machine. Otherwise, finish the edges following directions for your particular project.

Mount the embroidery in one of two ways: use heavy cardboard for small pieces, and artist's stretcher strips or plywood for larger ones. Be sure corners of stretcher strips are square; stabilize them with corrugated fasteners. Mark corners of plywood or cardboard with a T-square to be sure they are right angles.

Soften the appearance of the embroidery against a hard backing by padding with quilt batting, thin foam, or fleece cut to size.

Lay blocked embroidery face down and center padding over it. (If desired, baste around outlines of the finished piece beforehand for easier centering of padding and backing board.) Center the backing board on top. Pull the edges of the fabric over the board, and staple or tack, starting in the center and working toward the corners. Keep grain lines straight.

When using cardboard, hold edges in place with tape. Then, using heavy-duty thread, sew the raw edges together with long zigzag stitches from top to bottom and side to side. Remove tape.

Color Key
A Silver
B White
C Black

Stitch Key
1 Chain stitch
2 Long-and-short stitch
3 French knot (loose)
4 Leaf stitch
5 Outline stitch
6 Satin stitch

Sew transparent beads in clusters of three on the JOY as indicated. Use smaller, pearly beads in circles and between the two angels.

Tambour Work—Mediterranean Pillow

Tambour work is chain stitched embroidery done with a crochet hook. Designs with large areas of solid filling can be worked quickly, easily, and attractively in this unusual technique.

While tambour work is often done with pearl cotton or another twisted thread, this design from Greece is worked in soft wools.

Materials
26x26 inches of white wool
26x26 inches of backing fabric
3-ply Persian wool in the
   following colors: white,
   medium and light copen blue,
   medium and light rose,
   medium brown, light
   gray-green, olive, forest
   green, and light and dark
   yellow
Embroidery hoop or frame
Size 7 crochet hook
24-inch square pillow form

Directions
The pattern is for one quarter of the pillow. Enlarge it, reversing as necessary, and transfer it to the wool. Mount the fabric firmly in a frame until it is *taut*. Use one strand of yarn throughout, referring to the photograph for color placement.

Anchor the yarn on the underside of the fabric and work with one hand under the frame guiding yarn over the hook, and the other hand on top working the hook. For each stitch, insert the hook into the fabric and draw up a loop ⅛ to ¼ inch long. Drop the loop off the hook. Insert the hook into the top of the loop just made, reinsert it into the fabric, and bring up the next loop. Continue in this way along the line of the design motif.

To master the sequence of motions involved in each stitch, you may want to practice on scrap fabric before beginning the pillow.

Outline each shape first. Then fill shapes by working from the outer edge toward the center in rows of chain stitches. For example, to work the round flower shapes on the pillow, first work the center dot in rose or blue. Next, work the outer edge of the petal shape in one row of white. Fill the space between the center and the white edge with rows of color, as shown in the photograph. Finish by working rows of chain stitches radiating from the central, petalled motif to the outer edge, as indicated on the pattern. Use dotted lines as guides for the length of the narrow "petals." Work rows close together, covering the background fabric.

Block the finished embroidery; sew the top to the back along three sides in a 1-inch seam. Insert pillow form and slip-stitch.

1SQ.=1IN.

Middle Eastern Pillow

In many tambour embroideries, the background fabric is completely covered with stitches—as in this pillow from the Republic of Kashmir.

For another design to work with a hook, see the pillow on page 14.

Materials

17x17 inches #22-count Hardanger
17x17 inches backing fabric
Size 7 crochet hook
3-ply Persian wool in the following colors: navy blue, cream, brownish-gold, dark and light gold, light nile green, gray, light teal blue, scarlet, dark and light rose, peach, brown, and green
Embroidery hoop or frame
15-inch square pillow form

Directions

Enlarge the pattern at right, reversing it for the opposite side of the design. Following directions on page 95, transfer the design to the even-weave fabric, allowing a 1-inch margin on all sides of the pattern for the seams.

Mount the fabric in a hoop or frame so it is drum-tight. If you are using an embroidery hoop, you may want to wrap the inner ring with bias or twill tape—either one will help the ring grip the fabric firmly when the tension screw on the hoop is tightened. Prop the edge of the hoop against a table while you work the design so both hands are free for the embroidery.

Work the design following the directions for stitching explained with the Mediterranean Pillow, opposite.

Use one strand of yarn for the embroidery and refer to the photograph above for the placement of colors. Fill in the flower shapes and the urn first. Next, work the vines, stems, and leaves.

Add interest to the navy blue background by embroidering some of it in rows of chain stitches that outline the floral shapes and the urn. But work those areas marked with dotted lines on the pattern (at right) in spirals.

Work the cream background of the border in rows that outline the floral shapes, covering the fabric completely.

Block the finished embroidery, following directions on page 78. With right sides facing, stitch the pillow front to the backing fabric in a 1-inch seam. Leave an opening for turning. Turn the pillow cover right side out. Insert the pillow form, and slip-stitch.

1 SQ.=1IN.

Stitchery with Shells and Beads

This shell-and-stitchery wall hanging is made from beachcombing finds. If you do not have an assortment of shells handy, purchase a dimestore collection and work them into this unique design. Most of the fun of this project is in the variety of stitchery techniques you can incorporate in your version of this handsome hanging.

Materials

5 sand dollars
5 half shells
20 seed pearls
Center shell (or group of shells)
Small mirror
½ yard off-white textured homespun fabric (background)
½ yard medium-weight muslin (interfacing)
¾ yard off-white, closely woven fabric (backing and edging)
Off-white yarn
16½-inch piece of ½-inch wooden dowel
2 large wooden beads
2 smaller wooden beads
2 finishing nails
Embroidery needle
Embroidery hoop
White glue

Directions

Note: The finished size of the wall hanging is 16x15½ inches.

Lay out the background and interfacing fabric (muslin). Assemble your shell collection and divide the shells by size into groups.

Begin laying out the arrangement with the center shell. Then arrange medium-size shells in groups of threes and fives around the center. Fill in the arrangement with clusters of the smallest shells and seed pearls. Leave a 3-inch margin around the design.

Mark the positions of the shells and pearls with pins or light pencil marks and remove the shells.

Set the fabric and interfacing into a large embroidery hoop. Attach the center shell first, as a guide for the placement for the remaining ones. If the center shell has a hole in it, attach a small shisha mirror underneath it (directions for the shisha stitch are on page 87). Glue shells in place before stitching, if desired. Attach them with free-form stitching and couching, using off-white yarn. (For stitch suggestions, see the Glossary.)

Attach shells with holes by bringing the needle through from the back of the fabric, up through the hole in the shell, and returning on the outside of the shell. Follow the natural ridges on the shells for interesting effects.

Hold shells without holes in place in one of two ways. On small shells, work a straight stitch across the width of the shell and bring up the thread again at the edge of the shell. Loop the needle around the straight stitch and reinsert it in the fabric at the rim of the shell, as was done on the half-shells surrounding the center of the hanging. Anchor larger shells, such as sand dollars, with yarn "crosses" or couching, using enough stitches to hold shells securely in place. Attach larger shells first, then add clusters of smaller shells and pearls. Fill in the design with loose French knots, chain ring stitches, long straight stitches—whatever your imagination and the shells themselves suggest by way of shape and size.

When the stitchery collage is finished, remove it from the hoop. Cut a 16x15½-inch piece of backing fabric and trim the face fabric and the interfacing to the same size. Baste all layers together.

Bind the edges with the remaining backing fabric. Cut two 3x16-inch strips for the top and bottom edges, two 3x19-inch strips for the sides, and two 3x5-inch strips for the central hanging tabs.

Fold each tab in half lengthwise, and press. Fold the long raw edges under ¾ inch. Blindstitch the folded edges together.

With right sides together, lay the top and bottom binding strips on the embroidered fabric; pin. Tuck the raw edges of the tabs between the face fabric and the binding strip at the top, positioning them as shown in the photograph. Stitch both top and bottom edges in a ¾-inch seam. Turn the edging back, and press. Turn under the raw edges of the strips ¾ inch on the back and blindstitch in place, tucking in the remaining short ends of the tabs.

Lay binding strips along the sides, allowing ½ inch to extend beyond the bottom of the collage. Stitch in a ¾-inch seam. Finish as for top and bottom binding strips, turning the raw edges under at the bottom. Turn down the fabric remaining at the top to make side hanging loops. Stitch across loops at top, as shown.

Slip finishing nails through small beads and then through larger ones, and drive nails into ends of dowel. Slip the dowel between the tabs for hanging, as shown.

Creative Stitchery Sampler—Moon Flowers

This delightful 32x36-inch embroidered painting entitled "Moon Flowers" is a challenging sampler piece. Here is your chance to perfect stitches you already know and experiment with new ones.

Use small pieces of purchased fabrics or leftovers from previous sewing projects to create this fantasia of embroidery and appliqué. As you stitch, adapt the design to suit your decor.

Materials
Note: Make use of any leftover fabric or yarn
1½ yards brown burlap (background)
¾ yard pink fabric
¾ yard coral fabric
Black, brown, and green fabric scraps
Scraps of pink velvet
Green and gold burlap
Pink netting
Assorted fabrics in shades of yellow and green
Off-white, brown, yellow, green, coral, rose, and powder pink pieces of yarn in different plies and textures
Two 32-inch artist's stretcher strips
Two 36-inch artist's stretcher strips
Thumbtacks
Tissue paper
White glue
Soil-retardant spray

Directions
Cut a 36x40-inch piece of brown burlap and hand-baste a 2-inch margin around all four sides to delineate the design area.

Enlarge diagram A on page 86 onto tissue paper and cut each outlined pattern piece from your choice of fabrics and colors. Because this stitchery is meant to be a sampler, a variety of colors and textures in fabrics and stitches will add much to the design. As you choose, bear in mind that the colors you select and the textures of the fabrics will influence the mood of your picture. Also keep in mind the materials you have on hand.

Apply a *thin* line of white glue around the edges of each cut fabric piece to keep them from raveling. It will dry clear.

Assemble a 32x36-inch frame with stretcher strips. Make sure corners are square and then stabilize them with staples or corrugated fasteners to keep the wood from shifting as you work. Using thumbtacks, attach the basted burlap to the frame along all four sides. This provides a sturdy working area as you experiment with the placement of fabric to make a pleasing arrangement of shapes.

Pin the shapes to the burlap as you decide on placement. If you are dissatisfied with the color or placement of a piece, cut a new pattern piece and replace the original.

When all the fabric pieces have been attached, remove the burlap from the frame. Hand-baste the shapes to the burlap, as shown in the top photograph on page 86.

Embroider the large pieces onto the burlap using any appropriate stitch. We used buttonhole, stem, chain, and straight stitches for the tree forms. Leaf forms consist of leaf, satin, buttonhole, stem, and chain stitches. Moon and flower forms contain backstitches and chain, buttonhole, French knot, and straight stitches. Several of the circular shapes contain a series of closely spaced buttonhole stitches that are threaded with a second color yarn. Add as much embroidery as you like, using any number of strands of thread to vary textures and emphasize color and form. Refer to the photographs opposite and on page 86 for ideas. (Those on page 86 contain close-up views of the stitchery.) See the Glossary on pages 90 to 93 for stitch how-to.

See diagram B on page 86 to determine the outline of completed embroidery areas in our stitchery painting.

These suggestions can form the basis for your own unique stitchery painting, but remember—there is much room here for individual expression. Feel free to combine different stitches and to improvise or change the pattern as desired. Alter the design to suit your own needs and preferences and to use materials you have on hand in your own workbasket of threads and fabrics.

Gently press the finished embroidery on the wrong side.

Place the stitchery right side down on a flat surface. Center the wooden frame on top of the wrong side, using the stitchery's 2-inch basting as a centering guide. Starting in the center of each side, pull the burlap fabric from the front to the back of the frame; secure the fabric with staples. End by stapling along the sides to the corners, pulling the fabric tightly as you move around the frame. Remove all basting stitches.

Protect the front of the stitchery with a light coating of soil-retardant finish. Add a purchased frame if desired, or make a frame of 1x3-inch boards covered with additional burlap as we did.

continued

Creative Stitchery Sampler—Moon Flowers *(continued)*

Basting the appliqué pieces

Working the embroidery

The finished result

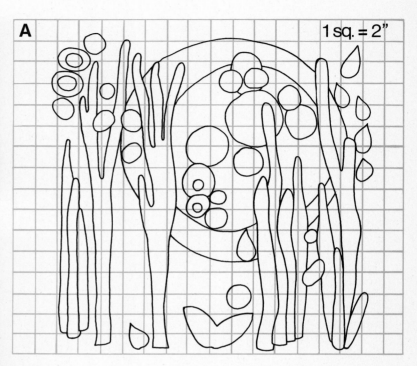

A 1 sq. = 2"

B 1 sq. = 2"

Shisha Stitchery—Embroidered Fish

(shown on pages 76 and 77)

Shisha mirrors from India embellish our soft-sculpture fish. Anchored to the fabric with stitchery frames, they are complemented by a variety of simple stitches.

Patterns are on the next two pages.

Materials

½ yard unbleached muslin
⅓ yard brown cotton
¼ yard each of bright orange, beige, and gold cotton
Scraps of rust, burnt orange, and sand-colored fabrics
Quilting thread
Polyester fiberfill
#5 pearl cotton in gold, yellow, bright orange, burnt orange, and brown
36 shisha mirrors
Embroidery needles

Directions

Enlarge the pattern pieces on pages 88 and 89, adding ½-inch seam allowances. Cut pattern pieces in the colors and amounts indicated on the pattern.

Pin the face to the front body piece, turning under the seam allowance on the curve (not the outer margins). Attach a shisha mirror for the eye, following the directions below. Use brown pearl cotton to attach the mirror.

Embellish the fish's eye with additional stitchery, referring to the pattern and to the photograph on pages 76 and 77 for color and stitch suggestions. Embroider the mouth and the curve of the face. Then set the face and front body piece aside.

Baste together fin #1 and its matching muslin piece (facing). Hand- or machine-quilt the two pieces together along the lines indicated on the pattern. Use pearl cotton for the quilting, in a color that contrasts with the fabric. Add embroidered French knot accents, as shown in the photograph.

continued

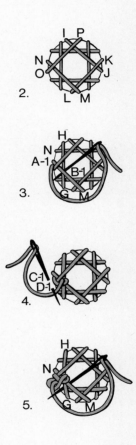

Shisha Stitch

1. Hold the shisha mirror in place with your finger or a dot of glue. Bring the thread up at A, close to the mirror, and down at B. Continue, following the diagram at right, to make a square of stitches over the mirror that secure it to the fabric.
2. Repeat the four stitches above, making a second square diagonal to the first. The two squares make the frame holding the mirror.
3. Bring the thread up close to the edge of the mirror and loop it around the threads of the frame making a stitch similar to a buttonhole stitch. Pull the thread tight.
4. Take a small stitch in the fabric along the edge of the mirror, as shown. Hold the thread under the needle.
5. Wrap the thread around the frame again, as in step 3.
6. Tack into the fabric along the edge of the mirror again, placing this stitch next to the stitch made in step 4.

Continue making stitches around the mirror, following steps 5 and 6. Be sure to pull the thread snug with each stitch.

Shisha Stitchery—Embroidered Fish *(continued)*

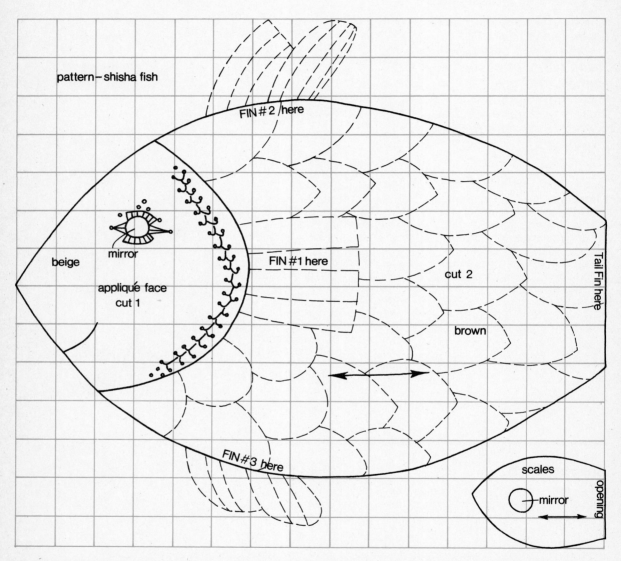

pattern—shisha fish

FIN #2 here

beige

mirror

appliqué face
cut 1

FIN #1 here

cut 2

brown

Tail Fin here

FIN #3 here

scales

mirror

opening

Next, trapunto-quilt individual sections of the fin, referring to the diagram at left, if necessary. In the center of each section, make a slit through the muslin only—not through the face fabric—and stuff lightly. Use an orange stick to push stuffing gently into corners, if necessary. Slip-stitch the opening.

With right sides facing, sew together the front and back fin #1 pieces, leaving the end open. Clip the curves and turn right side out. Stuff lightly and baste the fin closed along the seam line of the opening.

Before stitching the front pieces to the backs, complete fins #2 and #3 and the tail fin in the same manner, adding embroidered accents and shisha mirrors (to the tail fin) as shown on the pattern.

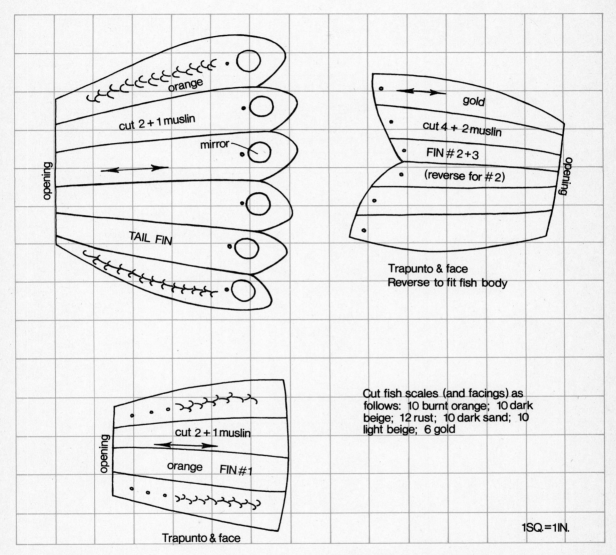

orange
cut 2 + 1 muslin
mirror
opening
TAIL FIN

gold
cut 4 + 2 muslin
FIN # 2 + 3
(reverse for # 2)
opening

Trapunto & face
Reverse to fit fish body

Cut fish scales (and facings) as follows: 10 burnt orange; 10 dark beige; 12 rust; 10 dark sand; 10 light beige; 6 gold

opening
cut 2 + 1 muslin
orange FIN #1

Trapunto & face

1 SQ. = 1 IN.

Stitch shisha mirrors to the tips of half of the fish "scales," as indicated on the pattern. Add additional embroidery to high-light the mirrors. We used French knots, buttonhole, lazy daisy, and straight stitches in a variety of colors.

Complete each "scale" by sew-ing a plain piece to an embroi-dered one, right sides together, along the curved edges. Turn,

stuff lightly, and slip-stitch the openings closed.

To assemble the fish, pin fin #3 under the facepiece, referring to the photograph if necessary. Sew the face to the body with running stitches, catching the fin in the seam. Baste together raw edges of face and body front on the seam line.

Pin the fins to the body front, raw edges even. Sew together

front and back body pieces with right sides facing, catching the fins in the seam. Leave an open-ing for turning. Turn the fish right side out, stuff, and slip-stitch the opening.

Using the photograph on pages 76 and 77 as a guide, tack scales to front, overlapping slightly. Vary placement so that two scales of the same color do not fall next to each other.

Basic Embroidery Stitches

Backstitch

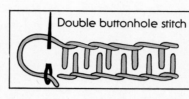
Double buttonhole stitch

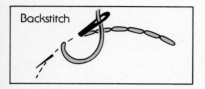
Braid stitch

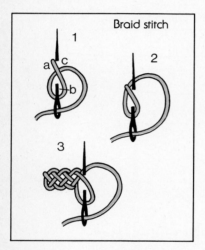

Cable stitch

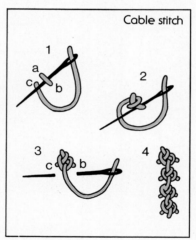

Buttonhole stitch and variations

Buttonhole picot stitch

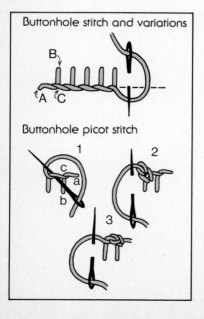

Chain stitch and variations

Cable chain stitch

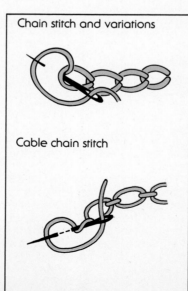

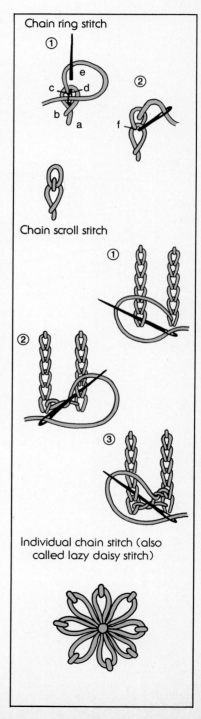

Chain ring stitch

Chain scroll stitch

Individual chain stitch (also called lazy daisy stitch)

Knotted chain stitch

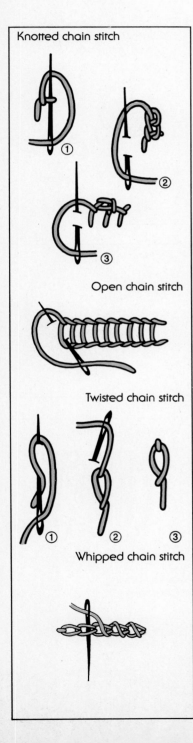

① ② ③

Open chain stitch

Twisted chain stitch

① ② ③

Whipped chain stitch

Couching stitch

Cross-stitch

Darning stitch (see also running stitch, page 92)

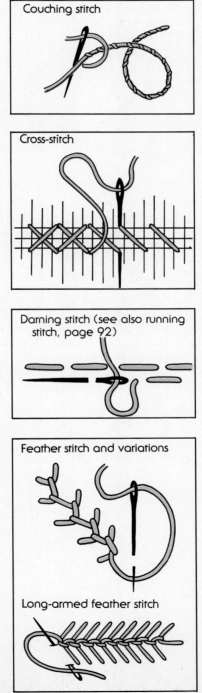

Feather stitch and variations

Long-armed feather stitch

Parallel feather stitch

Single feather stitch

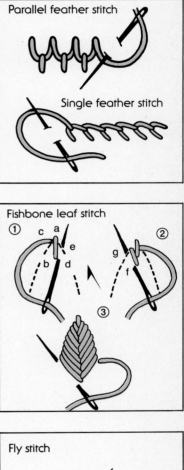

Fishbone leaf stitch

① c a e b d g f ② ③

Fly stitch

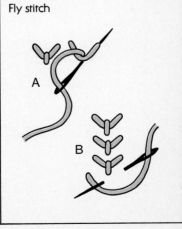

A

B

continued

Basic Embroidery Stitches *(continued)*

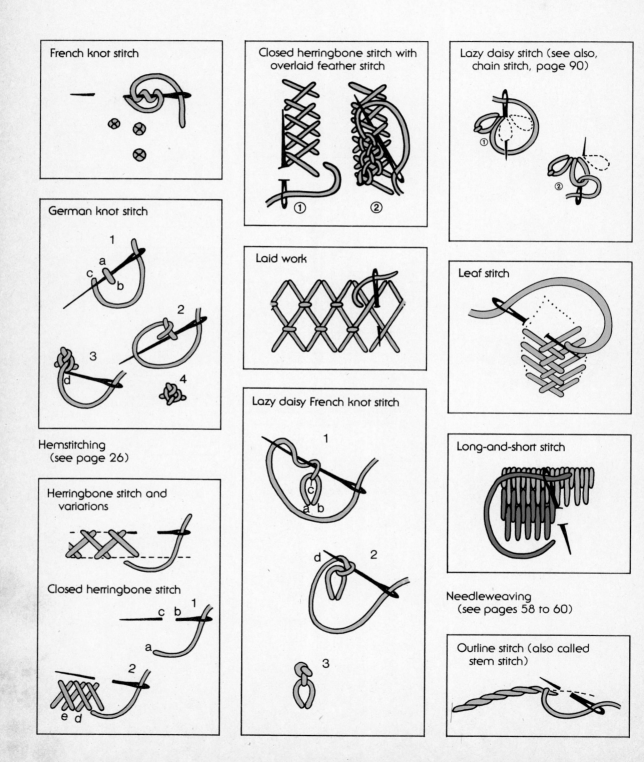

French knot stitch

German knot stitch

Hemstitching
(see page 26)

Herringbone stitch and variations

Closed herringbone stitch

Closed herringbone stitch with overlaid feather stitch

Laid work

Lazy daisy French knot stitch

Lazy daisy stitch (see also, chain stitch, page 90)

Leaf stitch

Long-and-short stitch

Needleweaving
(see pages 58 to 60)

Outline stitch (also called stem stitch)

Rosette chain stitch

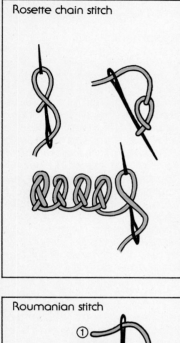

Roumanian stitch

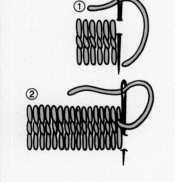

Running stitch and variations

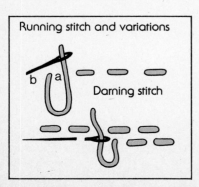

Darning stitch

Double running stitch

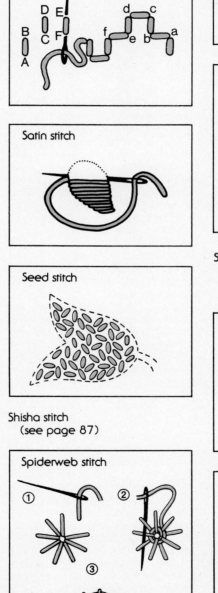

Satin stitch

Seed stitch

Shisha stitch
(see page 87)

Spiderweb stitch

Split stitch

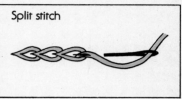

Star stitch

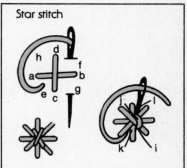

Stem stitch
(also called outline stitch,
see page 92)

Straight stitch

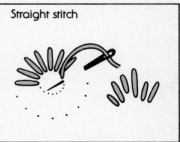

Velvet stitch

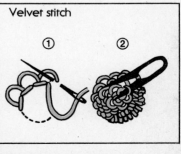

Waste knot
(see page 51)

Embroidery Materials and Equipment

Even-weave fabric

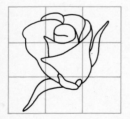

The original pattern

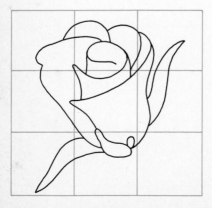

Enlarging on a grid

Materials

Unusual fabrics can make your stitcheries exciting, but the most commonly used ones for traditional embroidery are even-weave cottons or linens and other fabrics with a fairly smooth texture and a regular weave.

An even-weave fabric is one with the same number of horizontal and vertical threads per inch, as shown in the top diagram at left. The advantage of even-weave is that embroidery stitches will be uniform in size, which is an important consideration for cross-stitch and other counted-thread techniques. Aida cloth and Hardanger fabric are among the most widely available even-weave fabrics and each can be purchased with a specific thread count, such as 11 or 22 threads per inch.

Choose a good quality fabric that is firm enough to support the threads and stitches you intend to use.

Many yarns and threads are available for stitchery. Use wool yarns for crewelwork, and embroidery floss and pearl cotton for traditional stitchery. For special effects, try rayon, silk, and metallic threads.

Choose good quality, colorfast threads. If necessary, pre-shrink them by soaking in cool water. Dry thoroughly before stitching.

Cut yarns and threads into pieces about 18 inches long for embroidery. Longer threads will look worn and tired from being pulled through the fabric.

Yarns and threads have a lengthwise "grain" just as fabrics do, and are slightly smoother in one direction (with the grain). Thread the needle so you stitch with the grain and the thread will be attractive-looking longer.

Do not be afraid to use brightly colored yarns and threads. Colors will not be as bright on the fabric as in the skeins.

Store stitchery materials in a plastic bag to keep them clean.

Equipment

Keep both blunt and sharp needles on hand for embroidery. Blunt-end tapestry needles are used for counted-thread work and surface stitchery when the needle is worked into the spaces between threads or does not otherwise enter the fabric. The spiderweb stitch, for example, is worked with a blunt needle.

Use sharp needles for regular embroidery. Be sure the eye of the needle is large enough for thread to pass through easily without breaking. If crewel needles are too small, use chenille needles, which have larger eyes and sharper points.

An embroidery hoop or frame is a real boon to a stitcher. Mount your fabric in a large hoop, lace it into a needlepoint frame, or tack it to artist's stretcher strips assembled into a frame. When it is propped against a table or mounted on a floor stand, both hands will be free for embroidery (one on top, the other underneath). Your work will go faster and the tension on the thread will be uniform, reducing the amount of distortion in the fabric.

Among the small pieces of equipment many stitchers find helpful are *embroidery scissors* with sharp, narrow points, such as stork scissors. They are handy for snipping out mistakes.

A flexible leather thimble is useful to protect your fingers.

Commercial *yarn caddies* are widely available, or you can make one. Divide yarns for each project by color, and sandwich them between two layers of fabric cut into a strip. Baste together the layers between yarn colors, making a pocket for each. When you need a thread, pull it from the pocket. Remaining threads stay clean in their pockets.

Enlarging and Transferring Designs

When working with a pattern that needs to be enlarged or reduced and then transferred to fabric, choose the method that best suits your needs.

Enlarging (and Reducing) Designs

Patterns with grids — small squares laid over the design — are enlarged by drawing a grid of your own on tissue or brown paper, following the scale indicated on the pattern. For example, if the scale is "one square equals 1 inch," draw a series of 1-inch squares on your pattern paper to enlarge the drawing to the recommended size.

First count the number of horizontal and vertical rows of squares on the original pattern. With a ruler, mark the exact same number of horizontal and vertical rows of larger squares on the pattern paper.

Number horizontal and vertical rows of squares in the margin of the original pattern. Then transfer these numbers to corresponding rows on your pattern.

Begin by finding a square on your grid that corresponds with a square on the original. Mark your grid wherever a design line intersects a line on the original. (Visually divide every line into fourths to gauge whether the design line cuts the grid line halfway or somewhere in between.)

Working one square at a time, mark each grid line where it is intersected by the design. After marking several squares, connect the dots, following the contours of the original, as shown in the center and lower diagrams opposite. Work in pencil so you can erase.

Patterns without grids can be enlarged if you know any one of the dimensions of the final pattern. Draw a box around the design. Then draw a diagonal line between two corners.

On the pattern paper, draw a right angle and extend the bottom line to the length of the new pattern. Lay the original in the corner and, using a ruler, extend the diagonal. Then draw a perpendicular line between the diagonal and the end of the bottom line, as shown in the top diagram at right.

Divide the original and the new pattern into quarters, number the sections, and transfer the design as explained above (see center and lower diagrams at right).

Transferring Designs

Dressmaker's carbon paper and a tracing wheel or pencil are easy to work with. Use carbon as close to the color of the fabric as possible (yet still visible), placing it face down between fabric and pattern. Trace around design lines, using enough pressure to transfer them to fabric.

A hot transfer pencil also works well if it is kept sharp so design lines do not blur. Trace the outlines of the design on the *back* of the pattern. Iron the transfer in place, being careful not to scorch fabric.

A blue lead pencil is effective on light-colored, lightweight fabrics. Tape the pattern to a window; tape fabric over it and trace the pattern, making dotted lines instead of solid ones.

Basting is an efficient way to transfer design lines to dark, soft, highly textured, stretchy, or sheer fabrics. Use this method whenever those suggested above will not work.

Draw the pattern on tissue paper and pin it to fabric. Hand- or machine-baste around design lines. Tear away paper and proceed with the project. Remove basting when finished.

When design lines are faint, regardless of the method of transferring you have used, lightly trace them with chalk.

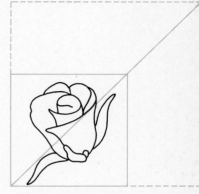

Enlarging without a grid

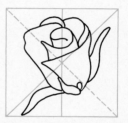

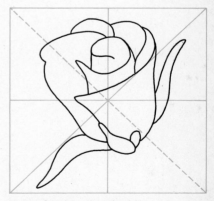

Segmenting the original

Transferring the design

We would like to thank the following people who have helped us greatly by contributing their project designs to this book.

Designers

Special thanks go to these people who shared pieces of embroidery with us, or who in some way contributed their talents to this book.

Acknowledgments

Make your home special

Since 1922, millions of men and women have turned to *Better Homes and Gardens* magazine for help in making their homes more enjoyable places to be. You, too, can trust *Better Homes and Gardens* to provide you with the best in ideas, inspiration and information for better family living.

In every issue you'll find ideas on food and recipes, decorating and furnishings, crafts and hobbies, remodeling and building, gardening and outdoor living plus family money management, health, education, pets, car maintenance and more.

For information on how you can have *Better Homes and Gardens* delivered to your door, write to: Mr. Robert Austin, P.O. Box 4536, Des Moines, IA 50336.

Better Homes ®
and Gardens

*The Idea Magazine
for Better Homes
and Families*